REFLECTIONS, RECOLLECTIONS & EXPRESSIONS:

Collected Essays

J.J. BHATT

Copyright © 2018 by J.J. Bhatt

ISBN Number: 978-1986646314

Title:

**Reflections, Recollections & Expressions:
Collected Essays**

Author: J.J. Bhatt

Visit:

Amazon.com/author/jjbhatt

Distributed by Amazon and
Kindle worldwide.

This book is manufactured in the United States of America.

O the
Supreme hope of
Reason,
Awake my moral sense
At this moment of
Existence...

(From: *One, Two, Three...Eternity*, 2018)

Table of Contents

Preface

Reflections, Recollections & Expressions is outcome of 23 essays I wrote in recent years. A few of them were published and others remained unpublished. I have brought them under one title, whence the birth of this book. Most of these essays are directional as they intend to share few ideas with the young generation while keeping an eye on the future. The remaining essays explore the integrated religio-philosophical point of view of Vedic and other associated thoughts defining the 'way of life' and general challenges and perspectives relating to human existence.

I believe life is a valuable opportunity to grasp the meaning of existence *via regia* individual morality and rational abilities. In a broad perspective, it is our noble vision, good conduct and sheer endeavor shall greatly define the future in the twenty-first century and beyond. It is said, we achieve what we believe, but we must diligently work toward it.

I am indebted to my wife Meena, children and big sister Hansa for their enthusiastic support. Also I sincerely thank Mr. Ram Cherkur for his technical help. Fortunately, number of colleagues, friends and students over the years have appreciated and helped me with my academic and writing endeavors to whom I deeply express my gratitude.

J.J. Bhatt

Photo # 1. The fascinating journey of my academic career began with young people in Fall, 1964 at Jackson Community College, Jackson, Michigan.

The Torch-Bearers

I bid avoir to all my worries and
I embrace the beauty of present
while I am in this blink of time.

In order to launch a helpful communication with young readers, I am going to begin with a brief statement relating to the essence of teaching endeavor. Fortunately throughout my academic career (1964-2007), I had an excellent opportunity to interact with over ten thousand students ranging in ages between 18 and 25 at various colleges and universities including in Michigan, Oklahoma, New York State, Rhode Island and Britain. An additional academic opportunity came during my retirement years when I taught the seniors in Florida (2008-2011); gaining a deeper perspective on the continued life learning experience.

As a backdrop it must be pointed out that my courses: earth and marine sciences with the environmental considerations were popular because it was perfect timing in the 1970s as three important events occurred in the United States: the creation of the U.S. Environmental Protection Agency (EPA), National Oceanic and Atmospheric Administration (NOAA) and the energy crisis leading to the overall emerging awareness of the environment, oceans and the planet earth to the American public, whence their great

interest to learn about main causes, consequences and possible solutions to the challenges on-hand.

At the onset of a new semester, in my first meeting with the students, I would seize the initial precious few minutes of their full attention, especially when their minds were fully focused about the general scope of the course and to learn something about their instructor; may be both while carrying some element of anxiety. I would try to ease the situation by congratulating them for making the wise decision to attend the higher educational institution. I would further assure them by declaring that they were the torch bearers of the future. Albeit they were the next generation of educators, scholars, leaders, innovators, entrepreneurs, thinkers, poets and creative artists who shall define the quality of human civilization; permitting necessary condition for humanity to live in a peaceful, stable and harmonious world. It was always exhilarating to notice their faces radiate with confidence as they became aware of their potential. I could see their faces registering a sigh of relief as if they realized the professor had validated their worthy decision to have enrolled at the college. They seemed to be buoyed by the hints of their potential role in the society.

I would continue to remind them that the university based series of tests and examinations were the first important steps, but the real pragmatic test would come in future when their professional journey would be best judged by what individual contributions (through scientific

10

Photo #2. In 1975, Students took six weeks Field Geology course to investigate the general geology of New Hampshire. Rain or shine, they worked very hard to meet their objective as each one of them presented excellent field research report and carried out a productive Q & A session.

knowledge and professional skills) they would make to build a better world.

I would usually spice-up my message by citing the famous quote: "We ourselves feel that what we are doing is just drop in the ocean. But the ocean would be less because of that missing drop." In first few minutes of a brief pause of silence, there was a tacit communication going on via body language between instructor and the pupils which plays even greater role in the overall learning experience of the very content of the given subject matter. Only when these two silent human dynamics: instructor and pupils blend well at deeper mental reality, marks the beginning of a successful intellectual dialogues between them. And that is where the real learning experience begins with an *espirit d'corp*.

11

One of the major objectives of **Geocean Society** is to raise the level of awareness and public education of our environmental issues in Rhode Island and southern New England. **Earth Day '92**, of course is one of the best ways to meet this goal. Therefore, every April 22nd is celebrated by our members at CCRI. In the future, the society plans to plant trees and shrub, undertake beach clean up and visit schools in Rhode Island to further expand the environmental awareness.

Photo #3A. Geo-class celebrates the "Earth Day." #3B. Oceanography class on a Beach Clean-up Day, Narragansett Bay, Rhode Island. . 1994.

Photo #4. Teaching has been my major mission. I thought it was the noble way to motivate and to fire-up the young collegian minds to think and to innovate new ways to keep the Planet Earth and its majestic oceans as a sustainable eco-system in the 21st century and beyond.

Once the students understood the rationale of their educational decision within the framework of the purpose, it was time to launch the formal presentation of the course material.

I had attempted to balance the course material among organized lectures, class discussions (conducted outside either over coffee chats in the cafeteria or outdoors when weather permitting, of course) along with laboratory studies and field trips. This multiple instructional strategies greatly facilitated in systematic exploration and understanding of the fundamental concepts and applications of their subject matters: earth-, marine- and environmental sciences. Moreover, it prepared them to conceptually and quantitatively grasp the magnitude of global pollution including the climate change, impact of natural disasters, societal need of natural resources (including mining of marine resources) and to seek necessary resolution through overall management policies relating to these issues as alluded.

My courses were designed to let the students boost their self-confidence with a solution-oriented attitude and of course through an active mode of learning which comprised: submission of a formal reports either a field work or a library-based research on a selected science topic of their choice. I attempted to encouraged student's to bring forth their communication skill by giving them opportunity to participate in regular class discussions. They were graded for basic theoretical knowledge, *in situ* field observations as a part of a report, laboratory report and class participation during Q & A sessions. In addition, there were the mid-term and the final examinations.

One of the great outcomes from students of oceanography in the 1990s was their joint workshop to put together seven volumes of Applied Oceanography. The publication included such timely topics: fisheries, sea-farming, mining of minerals, ocean management, ocean pollution, underwater habitat and

14

others. On completion of their team project, they looked satisfied and proud of their respective ability to accomplish something substantial and valuable. Once they understood fundamental concepts and applications of the subject matter were ready to go for higher studies either in sciences or allied fields.

Whenever my colleagues from sister institutions came to address the class, students were enthusiastic about the new mode of learning experience and were ready to ask relevant questions; never failed to express their personal opinions and dared to offer constructive suggestions how to improve either the growing threat of climate change or the impact of tectonic forces such as earthquakes having potential to trigger tsunamis along the Pacific coast. It was wonderful to see students actively participate in such discussion sessions expressing their self-confidence and their skill to logically communicating their ideas, concerns and opinions based on basic scientific knowledge and of course, understanding.

As an academician, I thought it was my responsibility to motivate students to discover their own potential how they can participate with their scientific knowledge and necessary skills to sustain a healthy global ecosystem in the twenty-first century and beyond. I attempted to convey my students that they were an important asset to the society, whence there was a true justification of their time, money and energy that they had   wisely invested toward earning a pragmatic but quality education.

15

Near the end of the semester, I would remind my students of Plato who had aptly said that good people produce good society, albeit they were the good people who were on their way to help build a better tomorrow. In this respect, they were indeed the *Significant Citizens of* the Planet Blue. Let them sing along:

Life Ahead

I am young
I am the future and
Got my courage to
Roll on the trail of
My big dream

This is
My time
This is
My mission:
To grasp
What I
Can become?

Let me be
Awakened
Let me know
My Truth for
This chance shall
Never be again...

BEING IN FLUX

Big things happens when people stand together
with a sense of inclusiveness and common vision
for a noble cause.

History has demonstrated it is from the pool of a few enlightened beings, great civilizations were built for example in the west, the City-State of Athens, Renaissance and later, the age of Enlightenment are noteworthy. In the east, there flourished great civilizations on the Indian subcontinent during the reign of Chandragupta and Gupta dynasties and in China during the times of the Chou, the Han, and the Tang dynasties to name a few.

These great ancient civilizations as alluded, irrespective of geographic locations were once nourished by the combination of benevolent ruler(s) working in conjunction with the dedicated priest class and leading thinkers of their time; guiding people to work toward unity of purpose and in cultivating moral values; permitting to sustain their respective enlightened society. So long their juices of good governance prevailed with positive religious belief and constructive intellectual input, each society enjoyed stability, peace and an impressive progress in various fields such as art, literature, philosophy, astronomy and mathematics and so on. In fact, each civilized society of the ancient time, left a valuable legacy behind their pragmatic knowledge and wisdom for subsequent generations to build on their own progressive society. However there is al flip side to the story of world's glorious past civilizations as in most cases, when unfit rulers coupled with the rise of religious dogmatism laced with xenophobic and jingoistic propaganda began as the dominant forces resulted in their monumental downfall.

Against this backdrop, it is equally imperative we must learn our modern civilization too is vulnerable to same fate like once glorified societies of the past, if we fail to apply our collective moral responsibility and rational dialogues to resolve major contemporary challenges: on-going rampant corruptions, erosion of civility indicating moral and ethical decadence, failure of the current educational system (failure in the sense this institution as a one body has failed to supply morally strong and ethically good students to the society) and the systematic neglect of the environment, especially the climate change of the planet.

The writings are already on the wall. Fortunately, the world community was awakened to the challenge of the climate change as demonstrated by the Paris Climate Accord 2016. Impressively, one-hundred and ninety-five nations participated agreeing there is an urgent need to address the issue of climate change, albeit for the very survival of human species and most organisms on earth. Unfortunately, the major nation of the United States of America in 2017 withdrew from the Paris Accord. At present, it is the general thinking that without the participation of the United States,

18

it would be quite challenging to meet the set climate goal as defined by the Paris Accord. Hopefully, the US policy on climate will change in the future and the world community will continue with its goal to address the challenge before it's too late!

Another big challenge emerges from the fact in the age of information is that we are simply talking but not listening to one another. In fact, our nonchalant attitude toward the futuristic consequences stemming also from the threat of nuclear proliferations, and the situation in Europe, particularly the rising tension between the NATO and Russian forces and on-going tense situation in the Korean Peninsula where North Korea threatens its neighbors and even the United States with its intercontinental ballistic missiles (ICBM). On top of it there is the religious- driven senseless conflicts in the Middle East and the issue of mass human migrations of the "climate refugees" from drought ridden nations of Africa forcing hundreds of thousands of refugees to flee mostly to Europe. Also, violent conditions in Central America forcing many people including children to flee to the United States and of course the war-torn people from Syria who have been displaced by the millions and many of them have migrated to Europe.

Revelation

Is it
Time to drop
The mask
Is it time to
Stop the talk,
And
Walk the walk?

Look,
Young blood is
Waiting for
Sometime to
Take over the
Helm
Let 'em have
Their chance,
Now

Time to
Drop the mask
Time to walk the
Walk...

(Poem modified from *Magnificent Quest: Life, Death & Eternity,*
Copyright © 2015 by J.J. Bhatt)

The Challenge

It is time we collectively attempt to bring together yesterday's geographically scattered wisdom of the world and steadily transformed it into *One Global Heritage*. The Global Heritage would be the expression of the dominant worldwide consciousness to foster a spirit of unity among seven billion plus people to coexist through understanding, tolerance and in sharing goodwill. In this context, it is imperative to realize we are the change: *Being in flux* struggling for the safety and survival of humanity itself.

Three Pillars to Rethink

**True spirit of freedom is
in our moral-self, indeed.**

The spawning ground for good citizenship begins first under the umbrella of a stable family upbringing and nourishing environment, followed by learning of a reason-based faith and in receiving a quality education. Specifically, in this essay, I am going to express thoughts on three major pillars: education, religion and politics that I believe together greatly define the potential outcome of a society.

Education

Plato thought it well that soul needs nourishment through good literature, beautiful music and philosophical truth. In modern time, it is the academia where young minds are further nourished with knowledge, to fine tune critical thinking, honing career skills and develop a solution-oriented habit. However educational preparation is not complete without the inclusion of necessary mental discipline of moral and ethical responsibilities to young men and women to become effective citizens. In this context, it should be the solemn civic responsibility on the part of the educational institutions to design set of curricula that would ensure supply of overall morally and technically-savvy productive

work force to the society. Specifically, youth with good quality of education along with moral habits would facilitate in realizing a balanced moral and material society in the 21st century. In this respect, accessibility and affordability to a quality education must be made universal to all citizens, albeit tuition-free to honor the human rights of young people in the 21st century. This is the direction; the educators must guide their curricula to realize a stable, peaceful and a harmonious society. It is the well-educated demography that has the incredible power to bring positive societal change.

Religion

John Gottlieb Fitche* lucidly spelled out, ".... religion is an important element in moral education of imperfect humanity." Moreover, I believe religion is an important psychological need of human beings that we cannot ignore, but it must be understood within the framework of reason.

In light of the on-going religious conflicts in the Middle East, North and West Africa and elsewhere resulting into carnage of many innocent people, it is time; we seek certain moderate religious reforms that would overcome the sheer insanity of "tribal mentality." It is time to initiate religious reforms along the basic rational and moral teachings that are

* *Attempt at a Critique of All Revelation* (1978, Cambridge University Press).

intended for the benefit of the global society and not just for the given glory of a geographically proclaimed god. Religious reform must be such that its teachings are free from heavy emphasis on rituals, worships and the pseudo-claims of superiority over other sister religions.

It is time, we as humankind understands that God is simply the guiding moral inspiration enabling the intelligent life to evolve from ignorance to the state of enlightenment. It is the enlightened citizens who have the godly power to promote harmony among people and of course with nature. If religious tension is abated, there would be corresponding dividend of peace, stability and security of human lives, especially for our children and theirs to come in the future. In that case, all geographically claimed god(s) would be transformed into One Almighty merciful Supreme Being who keeps looking out for His children's well being!

It is time to rejuvenate reasoned-based dialogues of inter-faith as a first step by allowing faithfuls of each belief system to honor the Universal Golden Rule: *Do unto others what you want them to do unto you.* In light of the fact we live in the age of information, it should be possible to re-educate the global citizens by sharing the common religious truth intended for the well being of humankind, *substratum.* Frankly speaking, religious understanding from a rational point of view is the survival kit, albeit it is a floating device saving us from drowning into the hellish state of violence, wars and genocides. The philosopher Voltaire aptly observed that the

24

human condition can be improved by eliminating superstition and fanaticism.

Politics

The eighteenth century thinker Jean-Jacques Rousseau wrote in his famous work *The Social Contract* about the concept of "general will." Rousseau proposed each citizen were to give up their natural rights and freedom in order to secure a collective sovereign power, the general will. According to him it is the general will of the people would have the power of passing necessary laws for the well being of the society as a whole. Essentially government is established to protect the rights of citizens. It is paramount that well educated and religiously liberated citizens fully participate in the efficient democratic process of ensuring human dignity, freedom and justice.

It is equally imperative that political and civic leaders seek out viable policies based on pragmatic goals and right mission to see that good citizens would be continually nourished with the spirits of tolerance, cooperation and inclusiveness. In this respect national and state policies must be also coordinated to lift the middle and poor classes since they are the backbone of a democratic society and main drivers of the economy.

It is from the vast demographic pool of the middle class the journey of making of an enlightened society begins. That is why quality and affordable education, open-minded meaning 'inclusive' religious teachings, free press, progressive tax system, honoring the Constitution and the voter registration are some of the principal core values that must be solemnly exercised to ensure overall stability and healthy functioning of a society. In this respect, the elected representatives must bear-in mind they simply are the servants of the people and not the other way round. It is germane to recall Abraham Lincoln's historic speech delivered in 1863 at the declaration of the Soldiers National Cemetery in Gettysburg, PA; assuring the healing nation, "...that government of the people, by the people, for the people shall not perish from the earth."

In short, the young generation of the twenty-first century must be made aware of the fact there is a need to reform the current status of education, religion and politics to fit the newly evolving reality of techno- driven civilization characterized by the emergence of a compressed world in the 21st century. In the broader perspective, the quality of life is determined by the collective will of the people, rational judgment and of course, commitment to build a society of peace, stability and harmony. In this respect, the young generation shall always play a vital role in coming years. That is why they must be validated today.

Let's Roll

Let's
Just kick aside
Ignorance and
Violence of
Our time

Let's
Focus on the
Noble mission
Of our time

Let's
Begin
The bold
Journey to
A good end

Let's
Roll the dice
To leave a
Safe future
for our kids...

THE DIGITAL SHIFT:
A Point of View

**Let the digital pursuit accelerate
clarity of "what-is-it-all-about"**

The reality of global consciousness must be the first step in launching a collective campaign by the young people to take on the pressing challenges of environment, nuclear proliferation, illiteracy, poverty, diseases and religious extremism to name a few. Against this scenario, it is paramount, the leaders, educators and ordinary citizens to utilize globally-linked digital communications system, which is yet to be fully applied for the benefit of humankind.

As a matter of fact the juggernaut force of modern high-level-technology is having its significant impact on humankind as the wide world is steadily transforming into a petite global village. In this respect, humanity if it is to survive in such a compressed finite world must learn to coexist with others bringing different set of cultural identity, religious belief and historic experience. In such a milieu of multicultural diversified society, we must launch a massive campaign of *digital education* enabling people to participate to ensure an economic growth which would sustain the core values of democratic ideals. In the same vein, many nations in Europe, Asia, and Africa will also have to come to grips with this new reality of coexistence with the people of multicultural backgrounds in the petite Global Village on their respective terms. The multicultural societal change is imminent in this techno-driven compressed humanity of the 21st century. It is time we give some serious thoughts to build a better future-in-making, today.

Toward A Digital World

Specifically, the digital education in the 21st century offers a great opportunity. In this respect, the best way to maximize the advancement of humanity greatly depends upon the knowledge-based opportunities such as free and easy access to the digital libraries: academic, public and private. In this context, Google's one time vision to build the first *Digital Global Library* is noteworthy. However, the big dream of Google's project did not materialize because of the copyright issue. However, in some way if that legal hurdle is resolved between the company and the authors and publishers, it would be a giant leap forward for bringing humanity together under one umbrella of *Global Education*.

At present, major U.S. academic libraries have already launched digital education designed to give free access to the students to all kinds of publications: books, articles, abstracts or whatever access to data as an illustration, the University of California at Berkeley has launched its *Digital Literacy Initiative* to develop 21st-century

29

information and research skills for students with a noble goal, "...to successfully live, learn and work in a digital society*."

Essentially, the digital literacy would promote factual information permitting to share our thoughts and point of views with others; leading to a better understanding, tolerance and adapting to the new reality of how to coexist in a multicultural and heterogeneous compressed world as alluded. When the digital literacy reaches out virtually the whole world, it would potentially lift humankind to get off of the curse of the on-going violence, hatred, wars and in extreme case, genocides. It is time we think of "not walls but digital bridges." However, the question remains, if the global-citizens are willing to take the first step toward a positive digital literacy?

Looking from a futuristic point of view, the *Digital Global literacy* would provide an unprecedented opportunity to spark "Global Consciousness;" encouraging global citizens not only to understand the narratives of their own history, culture , religion and so on, but more important, through rational knowledge learn how to survive as one humanity.

* *Fiat Lux*, Summer2007, University of California, Berkeley.

Time's Up

We're the
Global Internet
Unity of One,
Today!

Let us get
Ready to meet
Challenges of
Our time
Let us
Awaken
The spirit of
Goodwill
To meet our
Noble dream

Let us
Begin a new
Journey to the
Digital realm
To be
Well-informed
Citizens
At this time...

CONSEQUENTIAL BEING:

**Let young minds probe the beauty and truth of
"Who they are and what can they become."**

We live in a highly interconnected world today and what goes around in any part of the world must be the concern of whole of humanity. In fact we are the emergent *Global Citizens* manifest *Consequential being* in light of the on-going world-wide conflicts, an exponentially growing technological impact and the steadily increasing human migrations along with the serious environmental concern, especially in regards to the climate change. It is against this backdrop, we must emphasize to bring about a quality of education, constructive belief system and common sense to become aware of how to save our global society, specifically from the systematic moral and ethical decadence and the corresponding environmental degradation. In order to seek solution to the current challenges, let us begin with a first step by focusing on the young people who will be decision makers of tomorrow.

It is in this framework as alluded above, I believe mentor's solemn duty is to reset the north compass of his pupils. In other words, a teacher's noble mission must be to bring forth young men and women's rational and moral dimensions to their best; firing-up their self-confidence to let them believe in their own abilities. Let the young people be

32

nourished via educational institutions for good knowledge, practical skills and most important, to strengthen their moral core values and logical thinking. It is in this greater scheme of things, educators will play an immensely vital role in guiding the young minds in their future endeavor to build an enlightened society. In this respect, all mentors are essentially Serpas who must help pupils to climb the Mount Everest of their "Big Dream." Moreover, it is pertinent in this respect that religious and civic leaders and various guardians of the society must design a viable blue print that would direct young people to cultivate disciplined habits of mind; effectively participating in-making of a stable and productive global society in this century.

Let the grooming of young minds begin at the family level during childhood, subsequently let it continue with the right guidance of mentors from K-1 to K-12 and further advancing through the college life which would greatly enrich their educational and social experiences. In fact, it is the symbiotic relationship between societal needs and youth preparation (of knowledge, skills and moral habits) would help in defining quality of their futuristic society, whence the young people are the consequential beings.

Let this ride be sum total of
Our collective will to discover:
What's the meaning of existence,
If not today, then when?

The Law of Coexistence

**Humanity's collective strength resides in
its unity and rational judgment.**

**The primary requisite of the Global village in-making is
the adherence to the Law of Coexistence which boldly states:
*There is no escape for humanity neither in the north nor in the
south, not even in the east nor in the west, but to adapt in order
to coexist to survive despite differences, modus Vivendi.* To
meet the stated first law, people must begin to *Think Global.*
The emergence of new brave world in the present century is
challenging for our existence. It is time, we let go our deep
rooted "tribal mentality "and embrace a pragmatic strategy
how to survive and succeed in the 21ˢᵗ century and beyond.**

**Although the petite global village of today is in its
embryonic stage, it is fast emerging in certain parts of the
world, for example in North America, especially in the
United States and Canada and similar trend is in-making in
Europe and other parts of the world. In this respect, only
reason, moral vigor and ethical conduct would be the
ultimate determining factors for our survivability on the
planet. The change is imminent and we must get ready to
welcome it with new attitude of openness. Hopefully
humanity at-large shall absorb this forthcoming change with
reason and compassion. Ralph Emerson in *Self-Reliance***

eloquently expressed, "...in yourself is the law of all nature....in yourself slumbers the Whole Reason." My poetic take is as follows:

Not prayers,
But endeavor
Not worships, but
Our will
Not talking, but
Walking
Shall be the
Winners in the end

Not ignorance,
But awakening
Not despair but hope
Not hatred, but
Understanding
Shall bring peace
In the end

Not doubt, but
Self-confidence and
Compassion shall
Save us in the end...

Poem modified from: *Magnificent Quest: Life, Death & Eternity.*
Copyright©2015 J.J. Bhatt

The Power within

Character is our true essence;
greeting the world with a smile,
self- confidence and hope.

The actualization of moral and rational abilities give meaning in lifting human dignity to the higher planes of intellectual, spiritual and social maturity. In this respect, character is the supreme motivation and genuine strength of human success and survival.

Character is everything

Socrates succinctly said, *Know Thyself*. For him one who possessed right knowledge and good character (that is virtues) has a better chance to make right choices; enabling him/her to live a productive and a satisfactory life. It would be helpful to the young people to cultivate good thoughts and follow right conduct that would strengthen their character. A person of strong character possesses understanding, thus deep insight into his or her self- concept 'who he/she is and what he/she can become."

Human character is build by regular practice of habits of

DISCOVERY

Keep
Coloring
Life with
Hope and
Love always

Keep courage
For challenges
Shall come always

Let you be
Aware of
Your essence
Let you be
Awakened
To your
Excellence

Keep coloring
Life with a
Good humor and
Quick sense of
Forgiveness,
Always...

Poem modified from *Triumph of the Bold.*
Copyright © 2014 by J.J. Bhatt

mind through a repetitive process of cultivating good feelings, good thoughts and good words that would help in emanating positive vibes: emotive, cognitive and physical to the world by way of interactions with others: family, work place and the society.

The process of habit building of constructive thoughts, words and behavior first begins at the family level, further strengthened through grasp of a rational faith and subsequently via quality education. In this context, parents, teachers, colleagues and elders all play extremely important roles in young person's life, especially during their formative years. It has been verily said we become humans by the humanity of others.

Cultivation of Habits

Major path of "being becoming" is derived from proper stress management: in-take of right diet, moderate exercises along with yoga, meditation, prayers, visualization, listening to good music, undertaking creative art work or poetry, reading books of inspiration, in getting enough sleep and having constructive dialogues with others that would set the motivation to be good; ensuring continued evolution of healthy mind, body and spirit leading to development of a strong character. As a result, the person evolves as calm, self-confident and a fearless individual. Ideally speaking, young people of character shall have immense potential to lift not only their own dignity, but that of the society as a whole.

38

Stairway to Rational Inspiration

Human existence is a discovery of his moral self.

This essay is a brief metaphysical journey into the conceptual realm of God, consciousness, morality, freewill, purpose and meaning of human existence. In fact it is an instinctual human drive to climb the ladder to the grand sphere of rational inspiration in order to seek the meaning: "what is it all about?" It is simply an enduring enchantment of our minds to make sense of why we exist? Let us explore some of these challenging issues which are primarily confined within the majestic realm of the human mind, only.

NOTION OF GOD

Broadly speaking, God is a mental-conception which is based on belief and accepted by most of humanity. However, His existence is rejected by the minority of atheists whereas agnostics have suspended their judgment either He exists or He does not. Traditionally, God exist either in a cosmo-transcending mode or as immanent in the world. He is viewed as a Supreme Being and to others God and Universe is identical. Moreover, God is believed either only one entity (monotheistic) or an expression of multiplicity (polytheistic). He is also defined as Supreme Creator or personal deity.

God's existence has been proven by these classical major

39

arguments: the etiological (requiring the first cause), the axiological (prevalence of moral values in the world), the cosmological, (order in the Universe), the teleological (existence of purpose in the world) and the ontological (very thought of God). The priestly elites hold that God's presence cannot be proved since His existence cannot be subject to rational demonstration.

The philosopher Spinoza thought if scientific laws explained all the workings of the universe, there would be no need of God. I believe the notion of God essentially is to serve as a psychological shield against anxiety, fear of death and/or any unknown that would be harmful to human existence. Paradoxically, the notion of God though created by human mind is beyond his comprehension.

I have always thought that at deep mental reality; God must be understood as a guiding principle that facilitates to realize our own essence as a moral-self. In this respect, God may be nothing more than rational awareness of once own morality; enabling to evolve as an enlightened being. Only the enlightened beings seems to have the supreme capacity to discover the meaningful convergence of belief, scientific pursuit and human as a cosmic experience, thus independent of any man-made conceptual divinity.

It is time we explore that the fundamental motivators in a human being are experience, reason and morality all projecting his moral self who is metamorphically

40

worshipped as God. Remember Jesus said, "Thy kingdom is within you." Swami Vivakanada also said, "Divinity is within you." Indeed the rational concept of God must be interpreted as our own moral being whose responsibility is to defend good against evil forces in the world.

Notion of Soul

Plato understood the soul to be the seat of the moral personality capable of self-direction toward good. While Aristotle thought the soul as the form or entelechia of the human being. I would consider the notion of soul to be the human potential that is endowed with moral and rational attributes. In other words, the soul is a moral consciousness of a human being. The great Vedantists Sage Shankara viewed soul or *atman* in a broader perspective of anthrocosmic link between *atma-Paratma* (Super Soul) in an attempt to demonstrate the unity of temporal beings with the Eternal Being. The soul is the innermost striving of the intelligent life seeking an Aristotelian *Eudaimonia* or the *sat-chit-anand* (Hinduism) which defines the meaning of ultimate happiness and self-fulfillment.

Notion of Religion

The thought process of human existence is historically governed by the religious teachings, philosophical explorations and scientific pursuits. Among them, religion still is a dominant belief which in general holds that human

41

existence must be understood within the context of the Divine Revelation, God's sacred words and through rituals and worships. These basic notions of religion constitute major narrations and interpretations throughout history by the special clan of geographically dispersed priests; setting the tone for billions of followers how should they consecrate their lives in the name of Almighty God who is sold under different brands, of course.

There are few notable differences remain among major religions of the world at the surface, for example in the western religious tradition of Christianity, human existence is defined by a strict "obedient to the will of God" as in the story of Genesis: God commands Abraham to kill his son Isaac. God did it perhaps to test the degree of Abraham's obedience to Him. In China, it is the "Mandate of the Heaven" governing the fate of a ruler, therefore his subjects, and on the subcontinent of India, the laws of dharma and karma are the principal determinate factors defining human conduct. However, when religions of the world are rationally understood, *substratum,* their original message to humanity becomes apparent: how to become a good human being for the overall well being of the society. In this particular respect, all religions share their common essence which is ethical. Our failure to grasp this simple truth has perpetuated ignorance, consequently leading to countless bloody wars and number of genocides throughout human history and sadly continues off and on today!

42

NOTION OF CONSCIOUSNESS

Consciousness is simply awareness of the self and the surrounding world. It is the conscious thought per se that involves thinking and therefore a state of immediate awareness of reality. In this context, George Wilheim Hegel wrote in *Phenomenology of Mind*, the mind must come to understand itself as the only ultimate reality. He sought the logical necessity in working out mind's coming to know itself by way of dialectic which involved a movement from thesis to antithesis to synthesis. As an example, in ancient time, only one was aware of being free (thesis) and when civilization emerged, more people became aware of being free (antithesis) and during the age of reason, many were free (synthesis). Hegel understood his dialectic from a metaphysical point of view as he identified movements of historic experience evolving from the old notion colliding with the new, as a consequence progressively expanding human consciousness.

The Vedic thought of India affirms soul or atman is the human consciousness and its logical extension is ultimately *atman* dissolving into the Super-Consciousness, *Brahman*. Brahman is a metaphor for awareness of everything-there-is. Brahman is the summation of totality of all awareness often referred as the pure consciousness. In this respect, Sage Shankara's notion of anthro-cosmic link, *aham Brahman asmi*, meaning, I *am Brahman*" lucidly spells out the purpose of life is to link-up the temporal (human consciousness,

43

atman) with Brahman (the eternal consciousness). I would take it to mean linkage between the finite human possibilities with the ever expanding possibilities; maximizing one's potential into full actuality by evolving toward the greatest sphere of awareness to grasp: "What is it all about?"

I believe all these ideas as alluded marks a marvelous journey of human spirit from the realm of ignorance to enlightenment.

NOTION OF MORALITY & FREE WILL

Morality is solid glue of the society. It is essential because it enforces a spirit of responsibility to ensure justice (fairness), dignity and intelligent, *sensu strictu*. In this context, a civilized society tacitly exercises morality through its rational faith, quality education and fair legal means; ensuring equality, opportunity and accountability to maintain cohesion and stability.

Broadly speaking there are different shades of morality: personal, social, environmental and economics and so on. The issue of morality emerges on the scene when human exploitations: slavery, forced child labor, women trafficking and cheap labor occurs defining the dark side of humanity. Human exploitation also surfaces when strong nations steal natural resources from relatively poor countries through imposing their military might, fraud, bribe or whatever illicit means... disguised as the old time colonialism and imperialism. Environmental morality arises when systematic
44

degradations of earth's vital resources: air, water, soil and climate are endangered because of ignorance, but mostly because of greed and self-interest of the decision-makers either in the big corporations or the government policies geared for political reasons and mostly it is both.

Personal morality is an instinctual action of intelligent creatures: "what ought to be done" regardless of what one may want or desire. The spirit of morality is embedded in all human beings, but carries different degrees of awareness. The Vedic view emphasized awakening of the moral self (atman) to respect the law of *Rit* (which is the universal moral code that operates independent of any divine agency) and carry out one's duty for the duty sake (that is *dharma*) as aptly pointed out in Bhagvad Gita.

Immanuel Kant in the west wrote about morality as the fundamental criterion in the form of *Categorical Imperative* which stated, "Act as if the maximum from which you act were to become through your will a universal law." For Kant, the categorical imperative is deontological meaning it is unconditionally operational under all circumstances. Moreover for Kant morality could be exercised by rational beings only. He also pointed out that morality of what is right, good or ought brings into the play the notion of "free will" which is a choice given to human beings either to carry out an action or not about something of a given situation or event.

Morality has been also differently interpreted by various thinkers such as Hegel understood within the framework of historic experience whereas Nietzsche saw it as the morality of the masses (*die herden*) and the master class (*die heren*). For Nietzsche morality of the nobility or the ruling class was to pursue adventurous life style independent of any religious restraints.

ETHICS & HUMAN EXISTENCE

It is true human beings are endowed with concern for others such as sense of care, feeling of guilt, love for parents and so on. All such responses demonstrate human nature is good and that means humans have ethical spirit. Specifically, ethics concern with right conduct for good life. There are two types of ethics: personal and social. The personal ethics is focused on the moral responsibility of every individual citizen whereas the social ethics is applied collectively to all able bodied citizens in the society.

In regards to the issue of ethics, Socrates is most prominent in the western culture who initiated to explore human nature from an ethical point of view by proclaiming, *Gnothi Seauton* (know thyself). For Socrates if a person knows himself well, it meant good ethics for a happy life. Kant's ethics is based on the principle of goodwill that is will that honors the moral law. *Bhagvad-Gita;* emphasized dharma as the ethical duty to defend good against evil in order to ensure cohesive, order and peaceful society.

46

Quest

Let
Existence be
Contextual, so
I can define my
Essence in this
Grand design

Let me
Look around
Let me discover
My truth so, I be the
Meaning into this
Grand design...

Modified from
Magnificent Quest: Life, Death & Eternity.
Copyright © 2015 by J.J. Bhatt, Amazon.

Wonderful Time in New England

**Every day is shinning with a
Yankee spirit in New England**

My wife and I along with our six-month infant arrived in the state of Rhode Island and Providence Plantation in August 27 of 1974 to begin a new life as I got the opportunity to teach at the college and to pursue research and writing at the university. As we drove through the US Highway 95 going south, the old industrial town of Pawtucket verily conjured up memories of Britain where I had spent post-graduate years at the University of Wales-Cardiff (1969-1971). We kept heading south about 20 miles to our destination to the medium-sized city of Warwick.

Essentially, Rhode Island is a city-state with Narragansett Bay as its dominant economic resource system powered by fisheries, tourism and myriad related recreational activities. Also, the Bay is the home of the Graduate School of Oceanography (GSO), University of Rhode where leading marine scientists worked. I taught day time and the evening at the community college during the regular semesters. However, it was at GSO where I spent my research and writing time (Photo #1).

48

Photo #1. The author with his colleague Dr. Collins at the Graduate School of Oceanography (GSO). June 2002. In the background is *R/S Endeavor*, a major research tool for the sole purpose of scientific exploration of the world's oceans.

   The Great Little State of Rhode Island gave me an excellent opportunity to teach and continue with research and writings for terrific thirty-three years; facilitating number of scientific and educational publications. Fortunately scientific publications also opened up opportunities for me to present my works before a few national and international conferences and to participate in

49

Photo # 2. The author (fourth person from left) with his colleagues while attending a six weeks workshop in marine sciences in California in June, 1993. It was a joint project sponsored by the National Science Foundation (NSF) and University of San Diego., CA. The purpose of the program was to strengthen the curricula of earth and ocean sciences at various U.S. colleges and universities.

various professional projects such as the U.S. National Science Foundation (NSF) which sponsored the marine science programs in California 1993 (Photo #2) and at Harbor Branch Oceanographic Institution, Fort Pierce, Florida in 1994. I must confess best years of my family and my career were built around in New England, notably in Rhode Island. Let me express my gratitude to the people of the Great State of Rhode Island for giving opportunity in making a very productive life with happy times!

50

Inspiration

In the
Northeast U.S. is
Petite Rhode Island
Yes, that pearl by the
Mighty Blue Sea
A realm of caring
Folks I've known
'Em for a long

That's the place
I raised family and
Built career alright
That's the land
Where sailing,
Fishing and clam
Chowder kept
Life so alive

Autumn foliage,
Azure sky,
Snow-white winters…
Nor'easters renewing
The Yankee spirit
Always by the
Big Blue Sea…

Poem modified from *Rolling Spirits: Being Becoming.*
Copyright © 2014 by J.J. Bhatt, Amazon).

LIFE:
An Eternal Learning Experience

**Curious mind is young and alert
irrespective of either time or place.**

After retirement in 2007, my wife and I moved to the sunny Florida. Fortunately, an excellent educational opportunity came up for me as my proposed two courses: *Dynamic Earth* and *Exploring Oceanography* were accepted at the Osher Life Learning Institute (OLLI), the University of South Florida (USF), Tampa in 2008. The OLLI/USF also accepted my third course which fell out-side the scientific box: *Human Endeavor: Essence & Mission*. I taught these three courses between 2008 and 2011. The last course as mentioned was based on then recently published my book by the same title.

***Dynamic Earth* was offered in spring 2008, 15 golden minds registered for the course. In our first meeting I informed the group that considering each of them brought to the class between 30 and 40 years of professional career experience, it meant they had collectively filled the class room with whooping 450 and 600 years of cumulative life**

experiences! In that respect, I told them we were all students of life trying to understand not just our physical world: the beautiful Planet Earth but more importantly, our humanity at a deep structure. That is how we kicked off exploration of our home Planet Earth: an elegant speck embedded in the magnificent Universe. In subsequent time, I adhered to the same motivation toward seniors taking two other courses: *Oceanography* and *Human Endeavor: Essence & Mission.*

I vividly recall one of my students in "Dynamic Earth" albeit was a senior colleague, Retired-Professor Jack Robinson, a man fully-energized in his mid-80s to learn in order to rationally understand his world with a deep insight. Jack was great help to me as it was my first teaching exposure before the OLLI Group. He took care of the class roaster and made me familiar with the USF campus. While the lecture session was on, Jack was a totally different person as he never failed to ask number of challenging questions. He always professed in a Cartesian fashion, "to doubt everything while in the search of truth." As an individual, Jack was a thorough gentleman and a very helpful human being. He also gave me the benefit of his long time professional experience for which I am indebted to him. Indeed, Jack and other equally curious minds were driven by their fiery passion to know the subject matter of the Planet Earth so well and that made my teaching endeavor very meaningful, indeed.

These highly motivated seniors paid full attention to all

basic facts of learning which greatly impressed me. Candidly speaking, these illuminated senior minds kept me on my toes, alright throughout the session. It was their limitless curiosity, but more importantly quality of their right questioning to seek scientifically satisfactory answers was very exciting to me both as an instructor and as one of the participants in the class room.

In my second course, "Exploring Oceanography" there was a petite lady pushing in her mid- 90s named Rose Mary who always sat in the front row and listen to me with fullest attention and took meticulous notes. Rose Mary once brought her daughter in her 60s to the class; a perfect "chip from the old block." Rose Mary was a *rara avis* as she was physically and mentally quite active for her age and she unabashedly kept asking Socratic style series of questions during the class discussions. I must confess her line of thinking was perfectly well within the logical framework. Ms. Rose Mary was indeed a great inspiration to rest of us (Photo # 1).

The third course, "Human Endeavor" was taught while my book on the same topic was in-making. I'd 13 seniors in that class. The Q & A sessions with the students also greatly helped me in refining the contents of the book. After its publication, I taught the same course but to a different group in following session.

Photo #1. The class of Oceanography at OLLI/USF. Note the Lady seated on the left of the author is Ms. Rose Mary (2009).

Personally speaking, teaching opportunity at OLLI was a wonderful experience as I kept learning at a deeper level about the issues that I had probed in the said book. Now looking through the rear mirror, it was the golden minds of OLLI at USF that turned me from a Group Study Leader into a student of continued life learning, indeed. What a pleasant reversal of my academic fortune!

55

Photo # 2. My affiliation with OLLI at USF (2008-2011) turned out to be very rewarding as it gave me better understanding of life and therefore a deep insight. Socrates said it so eloquently, "unexamined life is not worth living."

Photo #3. The OLLI Institute annually held "Faculty Recognition Day." I appreciated such an event as it gave my colleagues and me a sense of educational purpose and an inspiring spirit to be part of "One Happy Family."

BEING HUMAN

Human
What an
Embodiment of
Everything
He can be god,
A master of
His destiny, or
King of million
Whims ruled by
Many dreams

Yes,
He can be
Anything,
He
Wishes to be

Let
Courage
Be his truth,
Let
Goodwill
Be the
Journey of his
Noble mission
To be fulfilled...

(Modified from *Triumph of the Bold*,
Copyright©2014 by J.J. Bhatt, Amazon)

ESSENCE OF VEDIC WISDOM:
A Point of View to Consider

**We are the embodiment of all
possibilities: *we're born to become*.**

We are citizens of this magnificently techno-driven age of information, therefore we are inevitably bombarded daily with excessive data that our three pound brains cannot instantly digest it all. In fact, the heavy flow of processing data may well let us forget our identity, ethnicity and possibly our historic experience. It is against this backdrop, young Americans of India extract not to forget the understanding of the Vedic thought as a foundation of their own being and to be aware of their heritage, whence the purpose of this essay.

I always felt that once we remove the mantle of the complexities of religious ritualism, Idotory, the notion of multiplicity of gods and goddesses; at the core, the Vedic thought (thus its derivative, the Hindu thought) vividly illumines awesome power of morality and rationality leading to the highest state of enlightenment of a human being. In this respect, it paves the noble path toward building an enlightened society. Let us explore this fundamental thesis of

the Vedic thought by considering the following salient
features:

The Vedic thought along with its subsequently
evolved point of views: Upanishads, Bhagvad Gita and
Ramayana and others may well be brought together into the
super-seven guiding principles: (1) *Rit*, (2) *Dharma*, (3)
Karma, (4) *Syaaum*, (5) *Viragya*, (6) *Kshma and (7) Moksha*.
Let us briefly explore each as follows:

(1) **RIT:** Rit boldly states that there is a moral law which
operates in the universe independent of any divine agency.
The message of Rit is well conveyed through the classic of
Ramayana, the story of Rama, the God incarnate. As Rama
was born in human form, he had to obey the moral law of Rit
as he too like any other person had to face grief and joy, good
and evil (for example, evil is represented in his nemesis
Ravana, the Nine-Headed King of Lanka) and in conducting
his duty as a son, husband, brother and a king of Ayodhya.
In modern time, the concept of Rit is commonly expressed,
especially in an ideally civilized democratic society: "No
man is above the law."

(2) **Dharma:** The notion of Dharma stems directly from
the principle of Rit. fundamentally speaking Dharma means
righteousness. Also, it is understood as an individual's moral
duty. The whole thesis of *Bhagvad-Gita* is centered on the
execution of dharma that is performance of one's moral duty
is to defend good against evil. Krishna is the spiritual (that

59

is rational) voice reminds the material (empirical) being
Arjuna that it is his dharma (duty) to take a fearless stand
against evil when good of humanity is in danger. It is only
when goodness in human being reins; an enlightened society
becomes a reality. In this context, it must be also noted while
performing one's dharma, there is never a moral equivalence
between good and evil.

(3) **Karma:** Karma is the law of action and consequence.
When a person makes whatever decision or choice that will
determine its outcome either rewarding or punishing. By the
same token, it is equally vital when a leader along with the
support of the people collectively takes a right decision based
on rational goodwill and practical vision would greatly raise
the possibility of realizing an enlightened society.

Looking at the modern landscape, humanity is in a dire
need to change from its growing state of prejudice and
violence to stability, peace and harmony. It is pertinent the
world must be transformed to a rationally-driven and
morally propelled mind-set as soon as it is possible. In
absence of it, as the history has vividly demonstrated, the
world would continue to dwell into the state of fear,
insecurity and perhaps ultimate demise of its glorious
civilization, *que vie*.

It is time, humanity and more important, present day
leaders, guardians and teachers of the society along with
concerned citizens assume their respective accountability

that is the act of Karma to ensure a world of peace and harmony among people of the twenty-first century.

(4) **Syaaum**: The principle of Syaaum means, "Self-restraint", or Will Power. The virtue of will power has been well illustrated by such great human beings: Socrates, Francis of Agassis, Mahatma Gandhi, Mother Teresa and many unsung heroes. In modern time, humanity lives with an excessive taste of hedonistically oriented life style with their insatiable wants, consequently drowning into the sea of insecurity, fear and anxiety.

The financial debacle of 2008 is another quintessential example demonstrating what happens when excessive greed and selfish interests (that is manifest evil) ride over basic moral attributes of honesty, integrity and common sense (that is manifest of good), as a consequence adversely impacting the middle class and the poor of the society. Today's leaders and religious guardians must exercise restraint in their rhetoric's, especially during the fervor of elections and in delivering the faith-based emotive speeches tacitly emphasizing exclusiveness, dogmas and preaching intolerance toward people of different beliefs.

(5) **Viragya**: Also called "tyaaga" means detachment. It is also a psychological strategy to keep calm and cool composer of mind from extremity of grief and joy, life and death, good and bad and so on of human conditions. The Viragya is an age old human experience as it was practiced in the past by

61

the Vedic rishis, many mystiques and stoics.

In modern time, it would greatly help to get away from the constant barrage of information causing the disease of "digital processing" on a daily basis from TVs and social media and so on. By way of Viragya, it is possible to reduce the habit of 24/7 techno-addiction and seek solitude to reset our sanity; becoming healthy, creative and spiritually productive human beings. Otherwise in absence of Viragya, we are all going to go techno-nuts in this 21st century!

(6) **Kshma**: The principle of Kshma means "forgiveness." Kshma, the attitude of "Let Go" is essentially pure courage a person can achieve and that marks his or her highest state of spiritual maturity. In a broader perspective, Kshma is the most effective way to free oneself from the grip of the seven sin: envy, vanity, revenge, greed, selfishness, lust and ego. Kshma marks mental liberation from myriad-stress of human existence. Kshma enables one to flow like a leaf in the river of life, whereas those who do not must drag through its waters for having chained by vanity, envy, revenge, and greed and so on; subjecting themselves to *dukha*, meaning suffering.

(7) **Moksha**: Moksha is a state of moral awakening. It is the actualization of the six human potentials: Rit, Dharma, Karma, Syaaum, Viragya and Kshma. It is the highest state of awareness a person can achieve. In modern sense, Moksha is an activated potential which enables an individual to be a

62

great mentor, a great humanitarian and/or an inspiring spiritual beacon to the society.

These super seven Vedic concepts as alluded were valid over 5000 years ago and indeed they are still applicable today, if rationally understood and sincerely applied in real life. If the trend of multiculturalism is in-making, there would be a dire need for all citizens to learn how to safely coexist to ensure a stable, peaceful and harmonious society. If the citizens are enlightened with the power of Moksha, so will the society. It is in this context, fundamental understanding of the Vedic education becomes relevant, especially to the young digital generation of the 21st century.

Non-empirical
Being, Brahman is
An eternal existence
There is no claim
To his name just
His concept to
Comprehend

Moksha,
Essence of
The Vedic truth
Let us grasp it
Through our
Rational insight...
(Poem modified from *Rolling Spirits:*
Being Becoming, Copyright© 2014 by J.J. Bhatt)

63

ESSENCE OF VEDIC THOUGHT

* The Oldest Human Thought of over 5000 years and still valid in the 21st century as it continues to reach out to nearly billion people in the world.

* To what is One, sages give different names. Monotheism   firmly affirmed.

* RIT (R): Universal moral law (Justice) operates independent of any Divine agency.

* DHARMA (D): Duty or Righteousness.

* KARMA (K): The law of action and consequence, which is accountability of human conduct.

* SYAAUM(S): Self-restraint or self-control.

* VIRAGYA (V): Detachment from trivial matters including excessive material wants and desires.

* KSHMA (Km): Courage to forgive.

* M0KSHA (M): Moral Awakening or Enlightenment

$$R + D + K + S + V + Km = M$$

According to the above rational equation, Moksha, the moral awakening is sum total of Rit, Dharma, Karma Syaaum and Kshma leading to the state of enlightenment of a human being. Only the enlightened beings have power to discover purpose and meaning in life on attending Moksha.

64

Essay 12

Meeting of the Minds

Truth inevitably draws toward a rational mind.

As a backdrop to the western reader, it was Max Mueller who introduced the religio-philosophy of India to the west. He eloquently expressed it as follows:

If I were to ask what the human mind....has most deeply pondered over the greatest problems of life, and has found solutions to some of them which well deserve the attention even of those who have studied Plato and Kant- I should point to India. And, if were asked myself from what literature we who have been nurtured almost exclusively on the thoughts of Greek and Romans, and of one Semitic race, the Jewish, many draw the corrective which is most wanted in order to make our inner life more perfect, more comprehensive, more universal, in fact more truly human a life....again I should point to India.

Moreover, it was near the end of the nineteenth century and beginning of the twentieth, the great Indian spiritualist Swami Vivakanada introduced fundamentals of Hinduism before the *Parliament of World Religions* in Chicago (1893 in the west beginning with the United States and subsequently in Europe and elsewhere in the world. The American intelligesia of the time welcomed Swami's Vedic and

65

Upanishadic messages which led opening of various centers of the Vedantic Society in the United States. That was the beginning of international religio-philosophical constructive dialogues between people of India and the United States. Beginning 1960s, Indian thought became popular among young people and since then it has imperceptibly evolved as a part of the American and the global cultures. Today in the 21st century, however we need to continue with more vigorous interfaith dialogues from a rational point of view among scholars and followers of major religions and with an inclusive mind-set rather than adhering to the old conventional "tribal ways." I have attempted to explore this particular aspect in my previous publication, *Human Endeavor: Essence & Mission* (2011).

Mission

Time to
Build an
Enlightened
World of
Goodwill

Time to
Cleanse the
Mind from
Ever present ills.

66

An Integrated View from India's Soil

Human is his own moral potential to
actualize social order, progress and peace.

I am going to explore a few highlights of the major religio-philosophical thoughts: Vedic, Hinduism, Buddhism, Jainism and Sikhism as a single comprehensive and well integrated pragmatic strategy to build an enlightened society. Moreover this essay is written with a single objective of dispelling certain superfluous differences among these five belief systems as alluded. These five belief systems are selected since they were seeded on the sacred soil of India. In recent years, I have attempted to bring forth an integration of major world religions my previous publication: *Human Endeavor* (2011).

An Integrated View

Goal: To seek a purpose-driven life of enlightenment. Enlightenment means that every citizen must be an active participant in-making of a good society for the well being of all.

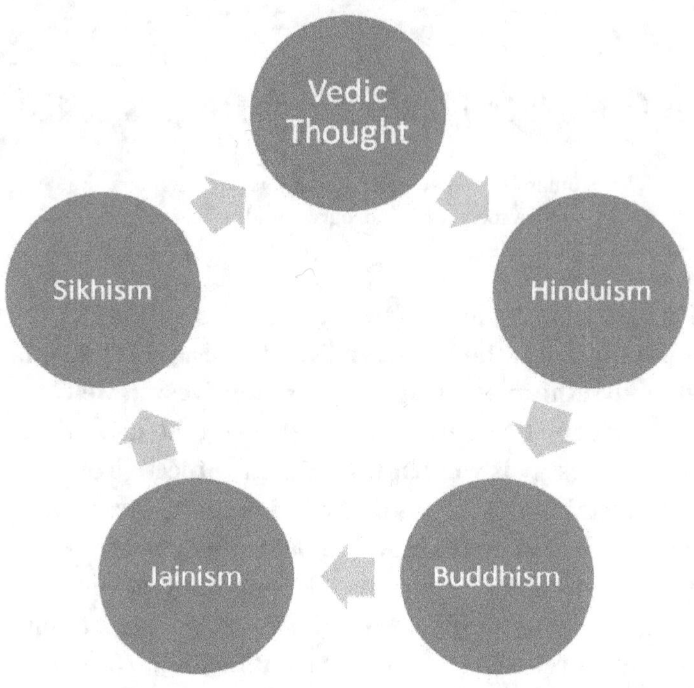

Figure 13-1. An integrated view of the moral inspirations from the Indian Soil. All five moral thoughts of India offered as a guide to hundreds of millions of people over the passage of time, how to acquire a rational understanding of life through discipline of mind, action and contemplation; gaining a deeper insight of "what-is-it-all-about?" and "what is our role in this astoundingly magnificent universe?"

General Scope: We humans are constantly striving, struggling and seeking to discover truth of our existence, "who we're and what we can become?" It is in this noble spirit, the Hindu rishis (sages) over 5000 years ago and later Buddha, Mahavir and Guru Nanak and other great awakened spirits attempted to guide humanity to evolve from ignorance to the state of enlightenment.

1. Vedic Thought: *Shruti, Smriti* and related 13 original *Upanishads* affirms that the laws of Rit, Dharma and Karma along with a disciplined mind of Syaaum (self-restraint), yoga and meditation would lead to Moksha; the moral awakening of human beings shall ultimately facilitate in fostering an enlightened society.

2. Hinduism: The empirical world is a theater of eternal conflict between good and evil. Each able bodied citizen's sacred duty (dharma) is to defend good against evil at all time in order to sustain a stable, peaceful and a harmonious society. It is therefore essential that every human being must assume his or her moral responsibility to accomplish this noble goal for the common good of humanity.

3. Buddhism: There are four causes responsible for human suffering and Eight Noble Paths to cure it. The aim of life is to liberate oneself from suffering and attend Nirvana, the moral awakening.

69

4. Jainism: To practice five vows to be liberated from bad karmas. They are: ahimsa, satya, asteya, aparigraha and self –restraint. The aim of life is to attend Kevala, the perfect wisdom.

5. Sikhism: Moral and ethical guidance from Guru Granth Sahib directs how to be a compassionate human being.

Wisdom Upanishads

Essentially, Hinduism's fundamental message is derived from the treasures of the thirteen original Upanishads and Bhagvad Gita. Two examples are cited as follows.

1. Brihadaryanka Upanishad (800BCE):

Lead me from unreal to real,
From death to immortality,
From the darkness to light.

2. Isha Upanishad:

Wake up.
Seek Truth.
Rise above
Ignorance.

70

Bhagvad Gita

Bhagvad Gita is an embodiment of Vedic Wisdom. It is comprised of 700 verses organized into 18 chapters. Its message is simple but quite elegant that all human beings must perform their dharma (duty or righteousness) to defend good against evil; ensuring sustainment of a stable, peaceful and a harmonious society.

ESSENCE of HINDUISM

• Not a religion but a way of life. It is essentially a rational blue print to let individuals assume their moral responsibility and good conduct to help build and sustain a stable, cohesive and harmonious society.

• Hinduism is based on four pillars:

ARTHA, KAMA, DHARMA and MOKSHA.

• Artha (economic security) + Kama (pro-creation/family) + Dharma (keep on conducting your duty)together leading to the royal path of Moksha (moral awakening).

• Pre-requisite: Discipline of mind: Thoughts, words and deeds and the practice of meditation /yoga are must.

• The Message: Hunman awakening is all about knowing your own moral self. Ideally, if all citizens are morally awakened, it is possible to realize an *Enlightened Society;* fostering an efflorescent civilization.

ESSENCE of BUDDHISM

Four Noble Truths:

1. Suffering exists in the world.
2. There are causes for suffering.
3. There is peace from suffering.
4. There is a way to overcome suffering via Eight-Fold Path.

The Noble Eight-Fold Path:

Right views, Right Resolution, Right Speech, Right Action, Right Means of Livelihood, Right Effort, Right Mindfulness and Right Concentration. Practicing of these Elight Habits of Mind over a passage of time leads to Nirvana.

Dhammapada
(The Path of Wisdom)

Buddha's teaching emphasizes moral and mental discipline, the four Noble Truths and the Eight-Fold Noble Path. The path of perfect wisdom can be comprehended by the following example:

Man should overcome anger by non-anger.

72

Buddha's Eight-Fold Path to Nirvana:

1. Right Views (*samma ditthi*) relate to an individual's knowledge of himself in order to achieve salvation.

2. Right Resolution (*samma sankappa*) expresses the need for an individual's full commitment to attaining salvation.

3. Right Speech (*samma vacha*) requires that the individual must not lie or commit any slander; otherwise his chances of attaining salvation will be wiped out.

4. Right Action (*samma kamanta*) requires that the individual seeking salvation must not kill, steal, or lie, must be chaste, and must avoid the use of intoxicants.

5. Right Means of Livelihood (*samma ajiva*) asks that the individual be engaged with an occupation that induces salvation, such as living a monastic life.

6. Right Effort (*samma vayama*) means that to succeed, the individual must exercise willpower.

7. Right Mindfulness (*samma sati*) requires that the individual engage in constant introspection to ensure that no misdeed or violation of the path has occurred.

8. Right Concentration (*samma samadhi*) requires the individual to contemplate the final truth as often as possible.

By exercising right views and right intentions, wisdom is nourished. By combining right speech, right action, and right livelihood along with right effort, right mindfulness, and right concentration; ethical behavior and morality are vitalized.

Essence of Jainism

● It affirms that karmas of desire and passion interfere with the quality of human soul. By discipline of mind, one would eliminate negative desires and passion; freeing the soul from bondage and restore it to its original perfection.

●The human soul purification is based on five vows:

Non-violence (*ahimsa*), (ii) truthfulness (*satya*), (iii) honesty (*asteya*), non-possessing (*aparigraha*) and (v) those who completely renounce the worldly life must observe celibacy.

● The lifelong practice of these vows would ultimately attain the highest state of knowledge, *Kevala* leading to the liberation of the soul from bad karmas.

Essence of Sikhism

● Purpose: To seek salvation through mediation on Divine power, *Nam.*

74

One Voice

Let's just take
Baby steps to the
Temple of
Enlightenment
Yes,
To the place of
Moral intention

That is
The realm
Where
Virtue is
The norm
That's where
Human shall
Manifest
To be Divine
In the end...

• To reinforce good habit of thoughts and words by reading
the sacred scripture: *Guru Granth Sahib* (Lord Teacher
Book) which is regarded as the living teacher. After reading
the Guru Granth Sahib, it is followed by *Kirtan* (prayers full
of devotional songs) and *Langar* (also an act of *Prasadam* by
sharing the meal with fellow human beings).

• Affirmation: To welcome equality of all religions and to
accept all people irrespective of their background and to
uphold the spirit of brotherhood and to be ready in the
service to humanity.

Final Thought

The five major faiths: The Vedic, Hinduism, Buddhism,
Jainism and Sikhism as highlighted mark the journey of the
human spirit toward enlightenment. It is this quintessential
message seems to have ensured India's overall unity and
stability through many fogs and frictions that have occurred
over the course of its long history. One of the major reasons
why India's unity remained intact is due to the collective
religio-philosophical outlook of these five rational faiths
without imposing any violent act of proslytization. These five
major belief systems unanimously affirms how to become a
better human being to appreciate the grandeur, the splendor
and the magnificent power of our own being, the Moral Self.

Spark of Enlightenment

An enlightened being is an indefatigable fighter against ignorance, arrogance and indifferent attitude of sinful minds.

Human being is an intelligent creature; therefore possess the potential to be moral and rational, whence got the ability to attain the state of enlightenment. An enlightened mind is one who is aware of the self and the world from his rational point of view. Enlightened being rejects religious dogmas, meaningless rituals and opposes forced proslytization. It is the illuminated human mind that has power to destroy ignorance, arrogance and indifferent human attitude. An enlightened person is the noble soldier who defends good against evil.

In fact individual who has attained the highest state of enlightenment takes seriously his civic and moral responsibilities in attempt to build a stable, order and peaceful society. In this context, enlightenment means those who are committed in achieving human wisdom for the good of the society. In the contemporary world, an enlightened person opposes slavery, female circumcision, hatred, violence and injustice. In short, an enlightened person is the sum total of intellectual, moral and ethical maturity enabling him/her to bring about positive changes in a society.

Enlightenment in the East

As an illustration, the spark of enlightenment struck the ancient rishis (sages) on the subcontinent of India who underwent circa 5000 years ago, an intuitive grasp of the meaning of human existence; a spontaneous insight of wisdom called *Shruti* which subsequently passed on orally from one generation to the next. The oral knowledge so realized was later written down as the Vedas meaning illumination or enlightenment.

One of the outstanding enlightened principles the rishis of the time realized was that of *Rit* which lucidly spelled out the universal moral law operating independent of a divine agency; giving complete responsibility as well freedom to human beings how to conduct themselves to live a meaningful life. As a result, there emerged two major concepts: *Dharma,* the human duty, or the righteousness and *Karma*, the human accountability. Later there evolved three more concepts: *Syaaum* (self-restrain), *Viragya* (will power) and *Kshma* (forgiveness). The ideals of Rit, Dharma, Karma, Syaaum, Viragya and Kshma together enabled an individual to achieve *Moksha* an experience of moral awakening, albeit attainment of enlightenment(also explored in Essay 13).

It is in the wisdom of the Vedic thought comprising *Upanishads* and *Bhagvad Gita,* we discover the fountain of enlightened inspiration. In subsequent times (sixth century

BCE and onward) it evolved into two major schools: the orthodox accepting the Vedic authority where as the heterodox rejecting it.

The Orthodox school accepted the authority of Vedic wisdom and was comprised of *Mimbasa, Nyaya, Vaiseska, Samkhya, Yoga* and *Vedanta.* Among these, the Mimbasa system was most conservative. The other five were focused on the meaning of human existence through philosophical inquires dealing with the epistemological, logical and ethical aspects such as the Nyaya and Vaiseika systems. The Vedanta emphasized the concept of *Brahman*, the eternal existence or often regarded as pure consciousness. The Brahman can be either *Nirguna* (One without attributes) or *Saguna* (One with attributes). The Yoga system is essentially a mediation technique geared for keeping mind, body and spirit to be calm and alert; maintaining an optimum healthy state of a person. Both the Yoga and the Vedanta systems are well known today in the world.

The Heterodox schools included *Buddhism* and *Jainism.* Buddhism probed the primary issue of how to cure human suffering through practicing the Noble Eight Paths: *right views, right intention, right speech, right conduct, right livelihood, right effort, right mindset and right concentration.*

According to Buddha if a person cultivated these eight habits of mind, in time would achieve wisdom, morality and mindfulness, thus *Nirvana*, the liberation from cravings and

79

negative desires. The Nirvana is the spark of human wisdom, albeit his enlightenment.

Jainism emphasized in cultivation of five vows as a means of liberation from bad karmas, meaning from the world of ignorance. These five vows are (1) non-violence (*ahimsa*), (2) truthfulness (*satya*), (3) honesty (*asteya*), (4) non-possession and (5) sexual restraint. The individual who masters these five vows in life ultimately gains *Kevala,* the highest spiritual wisdom, or enlightenment.

The rational of the Vedic, Buddhist and Jainistic point of views are essentially simple and elegant as they in their respective ways have enabled hundreds of millions of followers to live in peace and with a mutual respect throughout the history on the subcontinent and outside of it in Asia and many other parts of the world. These three rational systems of thoughts as alluded have taken themselves out of the religious based conflict on one hand, and asking their respective followers to assume social and moral responsibilities to ensure a stable, peaceful and harmonious world on the other.

Enlightenment in China

In China, *Confucianism* and *Taoism* along with integrated *Buddhism* marks the foundation of the belief system.

80

Confucianism is based on understanding of human nature and how to cultivate it to ensure social and political order. Confucius proposed citizens must cultivate their nature by adhering to three fundamentals: (1) *Ren* an attribute of human-heartedness or goodness. In a broader sense, ren concern with the well-being of all human beings in the society. (2) *Li* dictates governing one's conduct according to his social position. Li emphasizes extending reverences to others who are elderly or senior in position. (3) *Yi* is the principle which defines duty or rightness of an individual. For Confucius ren, li and yi lead to the social education and moral maturity of individuals; building a stable and peaceful society.

Lao Tzu, the founder of Taoism and an elderly contemporary of Confucius held *Tao* is the way, a metaphysical entity being the source of all things. Specifically, Taoism emphasized to live an authentic and simple life away from the artificial influence of social norms. Tao believes in flowing with the natural patterns of the Universe. Together with basic tenets of Confucianism, Taoism and Buddhism constitute the enlightened spiritual and social norms of the Chinese culture which has endured for many centuries and continues to prevail today offering hope and purpose in life to over a billion people in that big country.

Enlightenment in the West

In the west the foundation of enlightenment was sown by the Greek thought chiefly by Socrates, Plato, Aristotle and others. Socrates' famous quote: *Know thyself* is the emblematic of the western philosophy. However, in subsequent time, the intellectual movement shifted from Greece to Europe. For example during the 16th through 18th centuries, the Age of Enlightenment took hold in Europe.

The Age of Enlightenment essentially affirmed the supremacy of reason over faith. The new breed of thinkers of the time began to explore meaning of human existence, how to build a better society and overcome the religious rigidity that hindred the scientific progress. Major participants of the enlightenment were Galileo of Galilee, Nicholas Copernicus, Isaac Newton, Immanuel Kant, Rene Descartes, John Locke, Voltaire, and later came Rousseau, Hegel and others who directly and indirectly helped in defining the societal, political and scientific aspects of human existence in the twentieth century and continues to do so in the present century.

There was also an emergence of controversial figures like Fredric Nietzsche, Karl Marx and others in the nineteenth century. During the twentieth century, William James, John Dewey and others opened up the new school of American pragmatism based on the premise if an idea is workable, it must be applied to the betterment of human life. Also during

Spark!

Let's
Go after
Some thing
Greater than
Mere existence

Let's
Not stay
Divided into
This tribal
Cess pool

Let's
Not forget
The big
Dream

Let's
Summon
The Truth:

We are the
Global-One
Intent to live
In Peace...

the last century, there arose two major schools of thought: the so-called *Vienna Circle* comprised of the logical positivists like the leading thinkers Ludwig Wittgenstein, Bertrand Russell and others who mainly involved with the clarifications of the language. And there were the existentialists, for example Paul Sartre, Albert Camus and others who emphasized freedom over reason.

The twenty-first century is marked by the exponential growth of technology having unprecedented impact on humanity. Today, the globally-linked communication system via the internet and various social media has shrunk our world. Now it is possible for humankind to communicate ideas and its concern about common challenges and come to rational understanding of our world, particularly how to make it better than it has been before the present century. In other words, if technology can help us manifest as one awakened mind, it would be the first spark of true enlightenment of humanity; a definite step in the right direction to fulfill our final big dream.

An Intellectual Provincialism

Let us give a meaning to our glorious age of
information by tossing off all myopic ills.

Before the dawn of age of information in the 21st-
century, there prevailed a general tendency to break-down
the world into two spheres of thinkers: the eastern and the
western. So, we lived once and still we do so today in the state
of a balkanized mind-set.

The divided mode of understanding our world was
prominent during my student years in the 1960s and early
1970s, especially in the west. Moreover each sphere of east
and west had its own sub divisional identity: the English
empiricists, the continental rationalists and American
pragmatists. It was also true in the east, the Vedic scholars,
the Hindu thinkers, Buddhist monks, Confucians and Taoists
point of views to mention major ones.

In the western tradition, the general direction of inquiry
was described being reliance on experience, reason and logic
whereas those of the easterners were considered intuitive,
paradoxical and aesthetics. As a student, I was
uncomfortable to learn these subtle differences of our one

world of human thought.

In time as I understood the basic notions of religion and also having gained some insight into realm of the philosophical endeavors, Imean both in the east and west, I realized there was latent thrust of "intellectual provincialism." In this respect, I also felt that in the west, Hinduism was portrayed as an abstruse religion comprised of multitude of gods and being highly complexed ritualistic. I thought that sort of tendency persisted in the west for lack of full understanding of Hinduism in its total context of the Vedic, Upanishadic and Bhagvad Gita's messages to the world (refer to Essays 11,12 and 13).Hopefully, the contemporary age of information will change all such stereo-typed portrayal of any religion by allowing readers to have a direct access to its original intended perspective. It is paramount the Global young minds must be given unbiased information about a given religion; enabling them to make rational judgment through right understanding.

Potential for One World Religion

World's major religions although seem to express tribal-mentality in terms of different brands of God, unique sets of rituals, spiritual revelations and varying forms of worship on the surface; remain very much in agreement at deep structured mental reality. It is true that religion played vital role during the agrarian time when coordination of manual labor of many peasants and their management by the

86

governing authorities including the elite priests was necessary as a survival as well as overall well being of the community. Ideally speaking, each religion is an attempted moral and ethical educational tool to help create conditions of social stability, order and peace. Moreover each religion offers sense of belongingness to their faithfuls to share common values and cultural experience.

Houston Smith* succinctly spelled out: "When religions are sifted for those truths, a different, cleaner side appears." I do believe when we rationally understand the significance of *The Ten Commandments*, *Sermon on the Mount, the Vedic Karma and Dharma*, Buddhists *Eight Noble Path* and Confucian *Ren* (human heartedness) and Lao Tzu's harmony with Nature; expressing an ethical intentionality. Intentionality is directedness of consciousness toward a good end. When we grasp the real intention of any religion at deep structure, we realize world's religions together essentially addressing the issue of societal stability; an absolute necessasity of human survival in this otherwise insecured world fueled by fear and anxiety.

The religious trouble begins when guardians, leaders and priest elites failed to nourish constructive conditions, and instead tacitly preach exclusiveness, dogmas and pseudo-worship; producing zealots mercilessly killing thousands

---

*H. Smith, 1991, *The World's Religions* Harper, San Francisco

even millions as evident from the historic past. Unfortunately the religious driven fanaticism continues today. The end result has been disastrous for corrupting the universal spirit of goodness of humankind.

One of the expressions of intellectual provincialism emerges from the act of proslytization since it implies superiority of one religion over other. Moreover, in such an unwelcomed act of religious conversion, there is latent element of fraud as illiterate and poor people are lured through monetary help (understood by the local indigenous people as bribe) and telling them they are praying a false god. This has to stop, if the world inspires to be truly Global in spirit. Arnold Toynbee* said it well, "There is no one alive today who knows enough to say with confidence whether one religion has been greater all others."

The Intellectual Realm: Synthesis

In the realm of philosophical quest, great minds from eastern and western worlds have engaged to understand the purpose of human existence either within the framework of the religious belief system or independent of it. The fundamental notion of Buddhism in a way is not so different from the western existentialists such as Sartre's denial of existence of God. They have focused instead human beings to seek their own truth for each person is responsible in-making his own choice. The Carvaka system (one of the philosophical

88

schools of India) similarly not that different in genral from those of Hedonism and Epicureanism. The Vedic point of view shares number of basic ideas closely with those of Spinoza, Kant, Hegel, Schopenhauer, Emerson and others in the west. If the pattern of rational thinking at deep structure of reality is universal, then why promote the so-called, "intellectual provincialism" especially in the modern age of information?

It is time we the intelligent creatures learn to overcome these artificial barriers as alluded which are imposed either by the established instituted religious guradians or the influential elites. What we need today is an unfying force of Oneness. In other words, the present century is the best time to bring forth an awareness of the *Global Citizenship*. Let the young people with spirit of Global Citizenship discard the tribal mentality including the so-called "intellectual provincialism." Let them consecrating their lives toward making of a world wherein all people will live peacefully despite certain instictual differences, *modus vivendi*. It is said, individually we may live for a while, but we can survive collectively only!

In order to overcome the challenge of 'intellectual provincialism,' I suggest how about if we set up the *United Nations of One Religion.* Let the United Nations of One Religion bring about basic understanding, mutual respect and the sense of inclusiveness. Let this center be a beacon of hope to the young minds, to let them communicate and permit them to accept overall universal religious principles as the Global heritage of humanity. Let each religion teach them to accept certain local or regional differences but honoring the core values of each as an integral part of the One World Faith.

Awakening

When chaos
Prevails,
Myopic point of
View disturb the
Societal set up and
Friction begins

Whenever
There is a lack of
Rational dialogue,
Human liberty wanes

In such a milieu,
Superstitions,
Myths and religious
Dogmas sow the seeds of
Violence, wars &
Genocides, only!

.

(Poem from *One, Two, Three...Eternity*, 2018.
Copyright © 2018 by J.J.Bhatt)

Memories & Reflections:
A Journey to Remember

**The place where I understood the
meaning of "Light my knowledge."**

I am at the tail end of my journey and naturally it is good time to reflect and bring back some memories and certainly in this respect student years (1961-63) at the University of Wisconsin (UW), Madison was the beginning of my personal endeavor to go for the big dream that I could muster within my human capacity, of course.

While pursuing my graduate studies at UW, one of the first lessons I took it to the heart was what the great historian Plutarch who so eloquently expressed, " The mind is not a vessel to be filled but a fire to be kindled." Lo and behold, after graduating from UW, I had an excellent opportunity to teach nearly half-a-century to guide and to motivate over 10,000 young minds to explore the fascinating realms of the dynamic earth, its mighty oceans and the challenging cosmos.

---

*This essay was originally published in *On Wisconsin*, University of Wisconsin Alumni, Madison, WI, November 23, 2016 Issue. Its modified version is presented here.

My inspiration to engage in research, writing and teaching activities primarily was derived from great but tough-minded mentors and the quality education I received at M.S. University, Baroda, India; University of Wisconsin, Madison;, University of Wales, Cardiff, UK and Stanford University, Palo Alto, CA. These great learning centers laid the foundation of my career as a scientist, educator and an author. Needless to say great mentors, number of colleagues and scores of pupils have played an invaluable part in helping me to pursue my career-oriented mission. Indeed it is true as Sir Isaac Newton who aptly observed, "If I have seen further it is by standing on the shoulders of giants."

Well, let me express my deep gratitude via this simple poetic expression that I wrote over a half century ago while at UW. It relates to the Lake Mendota which is shinning jewel of the UW that has inspired over the years several thousands of young Badgers including my siblings, nephews, nieces and friends.

Lake Mendota

Enjoyed the sail
Through
Silvery waters of
Lake Mendota
In the year 1961

While
Sailing through
This realm of
Big dream

Suddenly,
We're jolted by the
Apoplectic waves;
Rocking our
Courage to its
Very core

We shrugged off
Fear and regained
Self-confidence in
An instant
Yes,
While sailing through
Magnifique Mendota
We reckoned our
Prodigious depth
Yes,
In that one instant…

Poem modified from *Rolling Spirit: Being Becoming/ A Trilogy.* 555 pages. Copyright © 2014 by J.J. Bhatt.

93

Splendor of Writing

**Writing is meditation that gives me
understanding, insight and solace.**

Writing what a solemn experience of solitude! It has always given me a passage to the unbounded sphere of ideas. Writing to me is a sort of mirror of my soul as I read in it endless possibilities of all there is to learn, to understand, to contemplate; gaining insight into the capricious human nature, the magnificent universe and in appreciating great minds of the world and their vision for the future of humanity and how the human journey be directed toward a noble end.

While writing, I am completely immersed in the wonderful state of meditation as I lose sense of my surrounding, time, place and everything else. Indeed, writing is an awesome experience of being in rhythm, melody and meaning of creativity driven by a turbo-charged inspiration. Certainly, to me writing is a veritable freedom to express, to communicate and to look forward beyond the quotidian life.

My passion for writing in various forms: fiction, non-fiction and poetry have been greatly motivated by the feeling to share my concerns and ideas with the world. In fact, writing gives me an opportunity to self discovery, in knowing my own inner being, albeit my essence as a living being.

I write to express what I think. I write to gain an ability to reflect, to discover what have I learned and through it, I like to share life experiences with others, especially with the young minds as they would be the torch bearers of the future.

During my active academic career (1964-2007), I wrote a few scientific texts and manuals and educational articles relating to the challenging issues of earth, oceanic and environmental aspects in order to participate in a collective movement of bringing basic awareness not only to the college bound young men and women but the general public as well. During my retirement years, my writings began focusing on topics concerning major societal issues, religio-philosophical point of views and major applications of scientific and technological advancements exerting significant impact on human existence notably in the twenty-first century.

I write to make young people become aware that they are born with an invaluable gifts of morality and rational capacities and possess the power to cultivate good habits of mind: good thoughts, words and deeds (making of right choices) not only to make their individual lives better but to greatly benefit their respective family, community and the society at large. I write to let the readers grasp the fact that only enlightened folks have the ability to bring about positive changes in the society.

95

This habit of writing also facilitated gateway to my introspection: "I am for what is the point of view of my existence, my ideas and my integrity as a human being." In fact, writing gives me an opportunity in knowing my essence. Moreover, the habit of writing has let me explore this fascinating world of hope with endless possibilities and opportunities to seek for enlightenment.

My fundamental message of writings to the young people: Always walk with your head-up and stand firm to honor your moral conviction and self-dignity. It is important to note that as a writer I do not attempt to convey truth but to awaken young minds to know their own truth *via regia* self endeavor, reflection and action. It is said, "If you cannot live longer, live deeper."

My Point

I do not write to
Earn notoriety
I do not care for
Wealth, power or
Fame out of it

I write to seek
Answer
To my queries
I write to fulfill my
Curiosity to know, to
Understand and to
Gain insight into the
Meaning of my
Own being

I write to
Express concern
Over
Issues of our time
I write to motivate
The young

I write for
Human dignity,
Global heritage and
Vision of tomorrow only...

Poem modified from *One, Two, Three...Eternity*.
Copyright © 2018 by J.J. Bhatt.

Human Endeavor:
A Retrospective Thought

**Human endeavor is an excursion:
"Who we are and what we can become?"**

I wrote my first literary work titled*: Human Endeavor: Essence & Mission* (2011) which pointed the way toward achieving an enlightened society in the 21st century and beyond. The content of it was drawn from the historic fountains of wisdom that comprised our global heritage. I considered such wisdom affirmed the power of rationality as the critical basis for the full realization of human potential. The primary message of the book centered on the main theme: *human can live alone but can survive collectively only*.

Human Endeavor essentially declared that humanity must fearlessly *Rethink Impossible I'm possible* through experience and reason, This message is imperative in view of the prevalent condition of human existence such as the issue of the religious- driven fanaticism, steadily growing nuclear proliferations, on-going rampant corruptions and the worldwide concern about the climate change and so on.

I wrote this book since it enabled to express my own worldview: the *Doctrine of Essencialism* and to offer some constructive suggestions to the young generation how to build a better tomorrow. In addition, I have written over 1200 poems comprising six books of poetica and a novel all intended to open up constructive dialogues among young people of the 21st century in the hope they will direct their attention with a solution-oriented mindset to build and to sustain a better world of stability, peace and harmony.

Will to win

Imagine, if we pour our
Collective moral strength into
This whirlpool of "Global potential"
We can move the mighty mountains
At will; crushing evil in
An instant

Imagine, just imagine,
if we streamlined
Our collective endeavor into sincere
Commitment; boosting power of goodwill
Across this globe... children shall
Say: "Thank you all for
Gifting a good life to live."

(Modified from *Rolling Spirits: Being Becoming.*
Copyright © 2010 by J.J. Bhatt, Amazon).

Excellence is a pursuit, Not a Destination

Let's not stand still and keep complaining. Life demands to explore, to seek perfection and to lift human dignity by building a better world.

Human being is a marvelous creature endowed with limitless creativity, propensity for moral action and yet carries evolutionary negative traits: envy, vanity, selfishness, greed, revenge, anger and false ego. If history is any guide, human beings have persistently demonstrated Janus behavior: at times shinning with good habits of understanding, tolerance and cooperation leading to a birth of a prosperous civilization. However humankind has also suffered from evil actions of violence, war and corruption; prompting unbearable condition of existence for the masses.

During the illuminating era of great societal maturity, moral and material progress remained at the zenith resulting into advancements in many walks of life as we know from major ancient civilizations of the world: Mohenjo-Daro-Harappa in the Indus valley, the Chinese, the Egyptian, the Mesopotamian, the Greeks and the Romans and others that bloomed in the subsequent times; all leaving us a lasting legacy of knowledge, wisdom and directing us toward

100

The Beat

I glimpse at the
Zillion stars shinning
So brilliantly in this
Grand dominion of
Cosmic experience

I am amazed by
This awesome
Inspiring scenery
That is
Awakening
My humble spirit

I,
Just a tiny speck
Who's
A celestial seed of
Eternity wandering
Into my 3-lb machine!

101

an enlightened society. However, when the dark side of human nature took over, it destroyed spirit of hope, love, and inventions; weakening the very fabric of morality. As a consequence in time dismantling all unifying forces of a vibrantly good society. Sadly, this has been the Janus autobiography of humankind; a very old disease of good and evil which continues to plague us today in the 21st-century. Isn't it time we begin to look beyond our present day dilemma, albeit our contradictory and paradoxical state of human condition?

It is time we begin to understand our collective responsibility. It is time, let us not talk more than necessary. Let us listen to understand one another in order to gain deeper insight into the solution of various challenges from the climate change to the cyber-hacking and those negative forces in between threatening our global heritage and if unchecked, our very survival as well.

Let us learn to adapt by accommodating our differences so we can strengthen our will to unify for a common goal of survival. Let us learn to walk the walk. Let us leave Myth of the Cave. It is time to live a purpose-driven life with an upward looking attitude. Let us pursue the path of excellence to meet our collective will to win.

ESSAY 20 *

ESSENCE OF HUMANITY:

A proposition for the young generation

We must be the pulse of the moment to leave
foot-prints of noble good before our time's up.

We as human beings must be aware of our respective strength meaning what is good and what is evil in us, thus make a concerted effort to eradicate the latter. Human weakness aka evil is eternally dancing into our thick heads in the form of envy, vanity, revenge, selfishness, greed and so on and outwardly manifesting as ignorance, arrogance and indifferent attitude; leading the passage to the world of hatred, violence, wars and in extreme situation genocides (as well illustrated by the world's historical record). To our chagrin, human scenario in a way is not much different than that of yesterday as if the past never quits lurking behind the present.

In this day and age of information, we are bombarded with constant stream of news: the climate change, nuclear proliferation, rising nuisance of religious extremists, severe impact of hi-tech and systematic erosion of civility, moral

Published in India Festival 2017, Tampa, Florida.

103

values and human dignity to name a few. It is time to introspect the future in terms of the societal responsibility that will fall on the shoulders of the young people in this century.

The hidden truth is we human beings are astonishingly powerful living forces of curiosity and imagination. In this context, our journey shall be worthwhile to discover: *who we are and what we can become?* To meet the challenge, we must begin with the knowledge that we are endowed with freedom of mind to think, to abstract, to create and to imagine. The very awareness that our creative human energy is the potentiality we posses in the form of moral and rational in essence that must be actualized through the vigorous practice of disciplining the mind: thoughts, words and actions (that is making of right choices). In time, it would be the martinet habits of mind shall actualize our deep insight: the value of human existence itself.

In the final analysis, human beings at the core are good, they have the ability to become the enlightened spirits. That is why it is paramount we must meet the challenge through our moral and rational capacities to know: "Who we are and what we can become"

Gratitude

Forgotten
Shadows of
Yesterday keep
Casting doubts
Even today

Time to kill
Ignorance
Time to
Illuminate
Human spirit

Life, what
A sweet song of
Happiness:
La vie esta belle
Life what a
Beautiful
Experience!

OH THE SWEET YEARS OF COLLEGE!

**Big dream and curiosity are
two hall marks of human mind.**

It is exhilarating to realize human beings have been driven by two powerful instincts: *Will to win* and *Self-worth*, albeit defining their purpose-driven journey while in this world. Specifically, to the young men and women of college years, it is the hidden energy stored as potential that gives them the belief there is something greater than themselves.

In light of the two powerful driving forces as alluded, college years are the best opportunity for young people to be nourished in career-oriented knowledge and necessary techno-skills and more importantly in bringing forth their individual moral, rational and ethical strengths. It is this combination of tools of economic survivability and cultivation of good thoughts, words and deeds (the last one referring to making of right choices and conduct); transforms them to be an enlightened individuals.

---

*Published in *City Masala*, December Issue, 2017, Tampa, Florida. A modified version is presented here.

The Pledge

You
May color
My life with
Grief or joy,
You
May color it with
Any challenge
To think
But,
I am here in the
Temple of learning to
Make some difference
In my life and for
The humankind
That I do care...

When young people share their moral and rational values with others like-minded, do they manifest as a formidable force capable of bringing positive change to the society. It is always the enlightened young minds that are capable of building and sustaining a great civilization. It is in this context life experience during the college years for the individual in question and collectively speaking for the future of the society is so paramount. That is why it is imperative;

we the grown-ups validate them to be the builders of the better tomorrow.

The real test of youth with college education as alluded shall become meaningful when they would in the future face the pressing challenges of our modern time such as ranging from geo-political tension among nations to the issue of climate change and many in between. In this context, today's collegians are the potential enlightened people of tomorrow who shall assume their societal and moral responsibilities; in making this world a better place for them as well as for the following generations to come.

At the end of the day, each generation must carry on the torch of hope and courage with moral sensitivity to ensure a safe, healthy and an all inclusive society. For this reason, let the young people well utilize their college years and not to miss this once in a life time window of opportunity. Mark Twain has succinctly expressed, *Sail away from the harbor. Catch the trade winds in your sails. Explore. Dream Discover.*

The Team Eleven

*Let the journey of human spirit offer a rational
understanding, deep insight and good judgment.*

Let us explore "The Team Eleven" which brings forth the eleven principles intended to begin a necessary conversation among young people about the challenge of how to lift the quality of human life. These are briefly presented as follows:

The first principle of life: Life is a bold human journey to interpret widening experience which would provide a rational point of view to liberate from the thick layers of ignorance, pseudo-sense of arrogance and indifferent attitude. It is only then a person enjoys his/her true freedom to reason, to contemplate, to understand and to seek solution-oriented measures to meet challenges of human existence and at that pivot, life begins to make sense.

The second principle of life: The purpose and meaning of existence must be understood within the framework that humans are spiritual beings born for human experience. This proclamation is well justified because we are essentially rational souls, we are intelligent beings and we carry moral dignity and freewill. The historic records shows great awakened souls such as Socrates, Abraham Lincoln, Mahatma Gandhi, Martin Luther King, Mother Teresa and

109

millions unsung heroes and a few benevolent rulers did walk on this earth to help lift the dignity of humanity. That is our global heritage, that is our collective inspiration and we must never forget it, but make sincere efforts to save it in the 21st-century and beyond.

The third principle of life: Human beings desire to live in a peaceful, stable and progressive world. In order to create a good society, it is germane that genuine civic and moral responsibilities be assumed by all citizens beyond their individual self-interest and greed.

The fourth principle of life: It is time we relearn to pay reverence to Nature by honoring our commitment to protect the planetary environmental resources: air, water and soil and the overall global ecosystem in the twenty-first century.

*The fifth principle of life: T*o appreciate the creative works of human beings: thinkers, poets, artists, scientists, educators, industrialists and humanitarians.... who are inextricably involved in their endeavor to give a meaning to our modern civilization. It is paramount the young creative minds be encouraged to progress not only in the dominant field of technology but to any field of their choice. In this respect, there has to be social and economic support systems to let them maximize the power of their respective...infinite imaginations and creativity; enriching the quality of human civilization to its best.

The sixth principle of life: Human beings must be committed in eliminating anxiety and fear that generates a sense of insecurity. For this reason, formal education and continuous dialogues among young people of different faiths, races and geographic origins be launched to foster greater understanding, thus to raise the degree of tolerance for a diversified demography. Let the young minds participate in volunteer works (as a part of their educational credits to graduate) to get a firsthand experience of how others notably poor live day to day. Such opportunity may well inspire them while holding decision-making offices in future to be sensitive to the needs of poor folks of the society.

The seventh principle of life: It is said, " character is everything," albeit it's the measures of a person's ability to take on great challenges with responsibility, or in providing reliable leadership and simply being trustworthy asset to the family, community and the society. Character is what gives an individual his moral strength. Good character energizes individual's moral and rational intentions and facilitates the right conduct. A person with good character has a better success than those lacking; opening the golden gateway to the enlightened state of mind.

The eighth principle of life: The essence of human being is his morality and that is what gives the power: "Born to Become." The inner strength of moral, rational and ethical attributes is a giant leap forward in the spiritual awakening of intelligent beings.

The ninth principle of life: Truth is the primary concern of human mind. Truth is a judgment which accords with reality. All human endeavors must be directed to unfold it. Truth is answer to one big question, "What is it all about?"

The tenth principle of life: The challenge to transform the ignorant human into an enlightened being is the rightful duty of the global citizens including their leaders, guardians and teachers. That is why right family upbringing, rational belief system, quality education and right guidance are collectively pertinent during the formative years of young people.

The eleventh principle of life: It is time human beings adapt to new technologies and at the same time sustained their humanity at all time. After all it is the humanity of others that strengthens individual's own humanity.

112

A GLIMPSE

Sum total of
All struggles
Means
Emergence
Of a
New vision

A new vision
Illuminates
Path to a
New reality

New reality,
In turn becomes
New challenge
And the cycle of
Challenge never
Ends

(Poem from: *Triumph of the Bold.*
Copyright   2014 by J.J.Bhatt)

Revolving Thoughts

**Let the young lead us toward a world of
peace, progress and enlightenment.**

Interestingly, creative artists indefatigably probe the
meaning of human existence from intuitive point of view
such as Picasso's abstractive work is noteworthy.
Philosophers have been looking into the essence of human
beings since time immemorial. In the 20th century, the
existentialist Jean Paul Sartre expressed in *Being &
Nothingness* that human beings fall into two categories:
Being-for-itself which is consciousness and *Being-in-itself*
comprised of everything outside of it. Sartre argues that
Being-for-itself is essentially nothingness meaning there is no
human essence, whence there remains his freedom. The
freedom means to make moral choices by individuals as their
own. In this respect, Sartre insisted existence precedes
essence. He also affirms that in a godless world, human
beings got no alternative but to choose; creating their own
values...albeit creating their freedom.

As a matter of fact, in life we continually navigate
through our quotidian existence between certainties,
possibilities and opportunities. In this context, it is germane
to let the young people evolve their respective point of view

via creative freedom; giving validity to their individual identity. Let young minds be validated for their powers of creative imagination and productivity. Let them enhance the very aesthetic value and overall dignity of human existence. I believe world enjoys the terrific tempo, rhythms and melodies of societal stability, peace and harmony when humanity is on the same page of knowing the truth of our collective survival depends on each other. Against this backdrop, I am presenting a few additional revolving thoughts to share with the young readers:

1.   I think hope is more significant than either love or faith. At the end of the day, it is hope that permits to float above the surface from the sea of suffering. Indeed, hope is the survival kit of each human being when understood from a rational point of view.

2.   Education in the 21st century must be geared to give young minds to develop and expand their moral strength, technical skills and the spirit of civic responsibilities. Only when rationally and morally motivated young professionals are supplied to the society, there is a better opportunity to build an enlightened society.

3.   It is time we recognize personal rights means assuming individual responsibility and not free privileges. Only when citizens are aware of their societal responsibilities over personal privileges and

rights, freedom has a genuine meaning to it.

4. Positive attitude lifts all human spirits like the balloons flying higher in the sky of endless possibilities since we are free from carrying heavy load of negativity.

5. It is time we the elders leave our permanent foot-prints of goodwill, hope and morality to the next generations, so we may mean something to them.

6. Awakening means identifying our moral self. The Moral Self is always experienced from our goodwill, hope, open-mindness, courage and humility.

7. It is imperative in life never to put ourselves in a position for failing to ask right question about a right cause affecting the nation's well-being.

8. Young people must live by the motto: *Trust thy courage"* Only courage helps in conquering anxiety and fear in life.

9. Integrity of mind means having self-confidence in one's own conscience.

10. Integrity must be also rock-solid in consistency to stick with the values and beliefs under all circumstances either favorable or otherwise.

11. Great souls are humble and full of compassion, but they are handful, whence there is so much injustice and misery in the world today.

12. The measure of a human being must be his commitment to a greater cause over his/her ego and self-interest and must be driven by a genuine passion to benefit others.

13. To acquire wisdom, one must drop the old habit of seven sins: envy, vanity, selfishness, greed, lust, anger and gluttony and instead embrace rational goodwill with the spirit of inclusiveness and in extending respect to others irrespective of their race, religion, gender or point of view.

14. The greatest accomplishment a human being can undertake is in transforming his potentiality into actuality. It is the transformation from ignorance to the awakened state of mind is the ultimate challenge of human existence. It is the awakening that reveals the purpose and meaning of life itself.

15. The *Win-Win* mindset is a noble goal, but requires lot of patience, preparation and cultivation of lasting positive attitude and optimism.

16. When caught in a tense situation and you are being humiliated, it is necessary to stay calm and unperturbed. Often silence carries big stick than a

brief burst of anger. Anger reveals weakness while calmness is expression of inner strength.

17. It is a pragmatic strategy to honor this simple principle: "To organize, simplify and enjoy life."

18. To keep life simple and meaningful means to let go the burden of seven sins(as alluded in # 13) and excessive material wants that support a hedonistic lifestyle. Instead time be put aside for meditation facilitating the cleansing of the mind.

19. In this grand material universe, enlightenment sparks only to morally and rationally driven beings. In this context, awakened beings are the most significant living entities capable of defining their destiny. They are the master of the universe for they have the capacity to achieve self-fulfillment and happiness.

20. Courage reaches its apotheosis when human is liberated from fear of life and death.

21. Moral aptitude and rational perspective enable humans to withstand life's vicissitudes with calmness and self-confidence; defining their true inner strength.

22. Human beings are living today in two parallel worlds: One is moral and rational and the other

corrupt and ignorant driven-by greed, envy and self-interest. As a consequence, the eternal conflict between good and evil is a fact of human state of mind since the time immemorial.

23. Human life is greatly defined by our will, our judgment and our moral strength and most of all, by our rational insight.

24. Human being alone exists as his ultimate quest for a rational comprehension of what is it all about?

25. Every individual must proudly proclaim, "This world is my rational point of view." Every individual must also claim, "This life is my endeavor to be enlightened."

26. The finite being is the invaluable gift of endless possibilities since he/she has the supreme capacity to transform from ignorant state of misery and pain to the highest state of self-fulfillment and happiness. At the same time, he must also watch out, life is but a blink of an eye.

27. Human existence is not a guaranteed package of either divinity or certainty, but an opportunity to cultivate moral and rational habits to build a better world.

28. Intelligent conversation opens the door for greater

119

understanding; gaining insight into the meaning of what is humanity's goal that would direct us toward truth.

29. In the final analysis, we must come to terms with truth that is our moral self, albeit it is our essence of endless possibilities; enabling us to arrive at the point of being equal of the Divine.

30. Usually it is the optimistic enlightened minds that bring forth necessary capability to build great civilizations.

31. We human beings are special cosmic experience since deep meaning of the world resides in our rational comprehension of it. Let the young blood sing their song:

If not for the young minds,
Who'll face the challenges of
Our time.

If not for the young genius,
Who'll know, if the journey's
Meant to be!

(Poem modified from
Magnificent Quest: Life, Death & Eternity,
Copyright© 2015 by J.J. Bhatt, Amazon)

Epilogue

Reflections, Recollections & Expressions is my attempt to share some of the ideas with the young people in light of the emerging new reality of the techno-driven civilization in the present century. My emphasis is to honor our global heritage and to appreciate humanity as an incredible unifying force.

The message to the young minds is that the world citizens are coming together under one umbrella of so –called "Petite Global Village." It is time to let go our old asinne thinking as well as conflicts fueled by the tribal mentality. It is time to appreciate human diversity: cultures, belief systems, customs and traditions for its the only sane and an adaptive strategy for the survival of our species on this astoundingly beautiful Planet Earth. Let us grasp the simple truth: we are all responsible in making our world a better place, so our children and theirs to follow will live in the realm of peace, stability and harmony.

What
An incredible is
This human journey!
An eternal poetry of
Rhymes, melodies and
Meanings...

(Poem modified from *Triumph of the Bold: a Poetic Reality,* Copyright©2014 by J.J. Bhatt)

Appendix A

BHATT'S SCIENTIFIC, EDUCATIONAL & LITERARY PUBLICATIONS (1965-2018)

(Textbooks/ books shown in bold fonts)

1. *Oceanography: Laboratory Studies*, 2002, Celecom Press, CT.

2. **Earth's History: Fossils, Time & Rock Record, 1995a, Celecom Press, CT.**

3. **Oceanography:** *Concepts & Applications*, 1995b, **Celecom Press, CT., 501 pages.**

4. *Undergraduate Faculty Oceanographic Studies* (UFOS), 1995c, NSF proposal written in co-authorship w/ Professor Mark Wimbush, Graduate School of Oceanography, University of Rhode Island.

5. Field Experience in Ocean Sciences: Coastal & Geological Oceanography and Marine Biology of California/Baja California, 1993a.

As a participant of the program submitted the report to the *U.S. National Science Foundation (NSF) sponsored Marine Science Short Course, Dept. of Marine Biology at University of San Diego, CA.*

6. Field Experience in Ocean Sciences: Coastal & Geological Oceanography and Marine Biology of Southern Florida. Johnson Oceanographic Institution, Fort Pierce, FL, 1994.a formal field report.

7. *Physical Geology Laboratory Manual*, 1993c, Celecom Press, CT.

8. International Pacific Consortium: An Organizational Approach to the Futuristic Resources System, 1990, PACON 90, *The Fourth Pacific Congress on Marine Science & Technology* Conference, Tokyo, Japan.

9. Oceanography: Year 2000 & Beyond: *Theory & Applications*, 1989, Celecom Press.CT, 370 p

10. Whales & Whaling: An International Perspective & Its Bearing on Conservation Efforts in Indian Ocean, 1985, Symposium, *Endangered Marine Animals & Marine Park, Biological Association of India*, Cochin, India.

11. **Ocean Enterprise:** *Resources, Politics & Conflicts,* 1984 a, Cambridge Int'l Press. Bridgeport, CT.

12. Digenesis in Main Limestone Series (Lower Carboniferous)in South Wales,U.K., 1984b, *The 10ᵗʰ International Conference Congress (ICC),*Madrid, Spain.

13. Marine Education: Futuristic Trends & Prospects, 1984c, Ocean *'84, Marine Science Technology Society,* Washington, D.C. 1984.

14. Pacific Resources Management: A Strategy for the future, 1984d, Research paper presented before the *First Congress on Marine Science & Technology Conference PACON '84,* University of Hawaii, Honolulu, Hawaii.

15. Diagenetic Pattern in Main Limestone Series (Mississippian), South Wales, U.K., 1983a abstract submitted to the *10th International Carboniferous Conf., Madrid, Spain.*

16. Multipurpose Offshore Mining System (MOMS) for the Recovery of Sulfur in Gulf of Mexico, 1983b, *OCEAN '83 Int'l Conference,* Marine Technology Society-IEEE,San Francisco, CA.

125

17. *Mineral Resources & Geologic Processes*, 1983c, V.1, Applied Oceanographic Student Workshop, CCRI, Warwick, RI.

18. *Energy from Oceans*, 1983d, V. 2, Applied Oceanographic Student Workshop, CCRI.

19. *Marine Fisheries*, 1983e, V.3, Applied Oceanographic Student Workshop, CCRI.

20. *Sea-Farming*, 1983f, V.4, Applied Oceanographic Student Workshop, CCRI.

21. *Marine Mammals*, 1983g, V.5, Applied Oceanographic Workshop, CCRI.

22. *Marine Pollution*, 1983h, V.6, Applied Oceanographic Student Workshop, CCRI.

23. *Underwater Habitation by Man*, 1983i, Applied Oceanographic Student Workshop, CCRI.

24. Marine Curriculum: A Pragmatic Learning Technique, 1982a, *OCEAN '82 International Conference, Marine Technology Society-IEEE,* Washington D.C.

25. A New Teaching Strategy for Adult Education, 1982b, *Conference on Strategies for Improving the Academic Skills of Our Student*, Rhode Island Group of Faculty Development and University of Rhode Island, Kingston, RI.

26. A Strategy for Applied Curriculum & Instruction in the 1980s, 1981, *OCEAN '81 International Conference, Marine Technology Society-IEEE*,Boston,MA.

27. *Physical Geology Laboratory Manual*, 1980, Modern Press, Cranston, I.

28. South Wales' Main Limestone Series (Lower Carboniferous): Application of Geochemistry to Stratigraphy, 1979, Abstract, *IX International Carboniferous Congress (ICC)*, University of Illinois, Urbana.

29. Applied Oceanography: *Mining, Energy & Management*, 1979a, University Microfilm International Publ. Co., Ann Arbor, Michigan.

30. U.S. Marine Consortia: A Contemporary Trend in Education, 1979b, *Sea Technology*, V.20, #9 (September issue).

31. Writer's Responsibilities, 1979c, an article in *Contemporary Authors*, V.77-80, Gale Research, Ann Arbor, Michigan.

32. Oceanography: *Exploring the Planet Ocean*, 1978a, D. Van Nostrand Co., New York, 322 pages.

33. Instructor's Manual for Oceanography, 1978b, D.Van Nostrand, New York.

34. U.S. Marine Paraprofessional Training, 1978c, *Sea Technology Journal,* December issue.

35. Offshore Technology: A Joint Program between University of Rhode Island and Comm. College of Rhode Island, 1976a, Report submitted to the *Board of Regents, State of RI/Department of Education.* Co-authorship w/ John Salisbury and Capt. Jeffery Mott, URI).

36. Geochemistry & Geology of South Wales' Main Limestone Series (Mississippian), U.K., 1976b, Modern Press, Cranston, RI, 110 pages.

37. Carbonate Petrology of the Upper Ordovician-Silurian Section at the Lone Mountain, Eureka County, Nevada, 1976c, *Journal of Sedimentary Geology*, Amsterdam, the Netherlands, V. 15, pp 172-191.

38. Geochemistry & Geology of Main Limestone Series (Lower Carboniferous),South Wales,U.K., 1976d, *Journal of Sedimentary Geology*, Amsterdam, the Netherlands, V.15, pp 55-86.

39. Environmentology: *Earth's Environment & Energy Resources*, 1975a, Modern Press, Cranston, RI.432 pages.

40. Evidence of Evaporites Deposition in the Lower Carboniferous of South Wales, U.K., 1975b, *Journal of*

Sedimentary Geology, Amsterdam, the Netherlands, V.13, pp 65-70.

41. Ti/Al Ratio as a Geochemical Index of Paleo-environment, 1974, *Journal of Chemical Geology* , Amsterdam, the Netherlands.

42. Ca/Mg Ratio Classification of the Main Limestones (Mississippian)in South Wales, 1973, *Journal of Sedimentary Geology,* Amsterdam, the Netherlands, V.13, pp 75-78.

43. Dolomitzation of the Carboniferous Main Limestones (Mississippian) Series in South Wales, 1972, *Ph.D. Thesis, University of South Wales, Cardiff,U.K.*

44. Some Preliminary Observations on Ca/Mg Ratio Behavior in Lower Carboniferous Limestone of South Wales, 1971, Article *in Mineral Exploitation & Economic Geology Proceedings,* University of Wales Intercollegiate Colloquium, Cardiff, U.K.

45. Microbial Action in Silicon dioxide- Calcium Carbonate –Water System: A Preliminary Research Report, 1968, *Geological Society of America*, Annual Meeting, Mexico City, Mexico, p.26.

46. *Cretaceous History of Tethys Sea,* 1967, Guymon Printing, Guymon, Oklahoma, 110 pages. Originally a M.S. degree thesis, 1963, submitted to the *University of Wisconsin, Madison, WI.*

129

47. *Physical Science Lab. Manual*, 1965, Guymon Printing, Guymon, Oklahoma, 120 pages.

LITERARY PUBLICATIONS:

48. HUMAN ENDEAVOR: Essence & Mission/ A Call for Global Awakening, 2011, Amazon /Kindle worldwide, 164 pages.

49. *The Seniors: A Wave Energy Still Rolling in the 21ˢᵗ*, 2011, publ. India Cultural Center, The Senior Club of Tampa on a St.Augustin, FL Trip.

ROLLING SPIRITS: *Being Becoming: /A Trilogy* Comprising over 500 poems, 2012, Amazon/ Kindle:

50. Book 1. *Spinning Mind, Spinning Time, C'est la vie*, 176 pages.

51. Book 2. *Meditation on Holy Trinity*, 167 pages.

52. Book 3. *Enlightenment*: *Fiat lux, 204.*

53 . ODYSSEY OF THE DAMNED: *A Revolving Destiny, 2013a,* Amazon/ Kindle worldwide.

54. Let, India Rise, 2013b, Poem publ. in *26ᵗʰ India Festival,* Tampa,FL, p.122.

55. PARISHRAM: *Journey of the Human Spirit,* 2013c,

Amazon/Kindle worldwide.

56. TRIUMPH OF THE BOLD: *A Poetic Reality, 2015a,*
Amazon/Kindle worldwide

57. MAGNIFICENT QUEST: *Life, Death & Eternity, 2015b,*
Amazon/ Kindle worldwide.

58. THEATER OF WISDOM: Essays on the Vedic
Thought, Human Existence & Futuristic Prospect, 2016a,
Amazon/ Kindle worldwide.

59. Essence of China: *Challenges & Possibilities, 2016b,*
Amazon/Kindle worldwide.

60, Essence of India: *A Comprehensive Perspective,*
2016c, Amazon/ Kindle worldwide.

61. *A Journey to Remember: Memories & Reflections*, 2016
(November), Wisconsin Alumni Association, Madison, WI.

62. *In the Realm of OLLI/USF Nation,* 2016, Unpubl. Article
written for Osher Life Learning   Institute, University of
South Florida, Tampa,FL.

63. BEING & MORAL PERSUASION: *A Bolt of*
Inspiration, 2017, Amazon/Kindle.

64. Essence of Humanity: a Proposition for consideration,
2017, *Festival of India* Annual Publication, Tampa, Florida.
131

65. Oh the Sweet College Years!, 2017, *City Masala Magazine*, Tampa,FL.

66. Life: The Eternal Learning Experience, submitted to *City Masala*, Tampa, FL, October 2017.

67. **REFLECTIONS, RECOLLECTIONS & EXPRESSIOSNS:** Collected Essays & Poems, 2018,Amazon.

68. **ONE, TWO, THREE...ETERNITY:** *A Poetic Odyssey,* (2018).

Appendix B

Bhatt's Recent Books: Synopsis

(1) **Human Endeavor:** *Essence & Mission/ A Call for Global Awakening* points the way toward achieving an enlightened global civil society in the 21st century and beyond.

(2) **Rolling Spirits: Being Becoming** is a trilogy comprising over 500 inspiring poems to explore, to introspect and to reflect, "Who we are and what we can become."

(3) **Odyssey of the Damned:** *Revolving Destiny* is a timely novel that dares to test the very mettle of human courage on encountering *tethe-tethe* with the super-intelligent aliens, the Gnocians from the far away galaxy, and much more.

(4) **Parishram: Journey of the Human Spirit** boldly declares, "Between birth and death, there's a mountain named 'Life' and it must be conquered with our shear human action, *Parishram* per se.

(5) **Triumph of the Bold:** *A Poetic Reality* examines major historic and contemporary societal issues within the framework of techno-driven global village civilization in the twenty-first century. The quest for the noble mission has been defined through the ages. But, the question is do we have a collective will to meet the challenge?

(6) **Theater of Wisdom:** *Essays on Vedic Thought, Human Existence & Futuristic* prospects affirms in the rational power of humanity to meet its challenges and evolve toward an enlightened society of the future by knowing "who we're and where we ought to be doing?"

(7) **Magnificent Quest:** *Life, Death & Eternity* is a collective odyssey of humanity to grasp what

is our purpose of existence and must understand what is beyond life and death *via regia* poetic imaginations.

(8) Essence of India: *A Comprehensive Perspective* brings to the readers an awesome 5000   years of a continued civilization beginning with the oldest Vedic thought to the modern day largest democratic nation with an eye on the future.

(9) Essence of China*: Challenges & Possibilities* explore the glorious Chinese historic past, contemporary issues and futuristic prospects. It focuses on the mindset of the decision-makers who have played vital role in-making of China in recent times and continues to do so at present.

(10) Being & Moral Persuasion: *A bolt of Inspiration* dare to remind that morality is a faculty of human mind which is directed toward achieving a noble goal of social order, peace and harmony.

(11) One, Two, Three...Eternity: A Poetic Odyssey is an explosive poetic expression that dare to probe into major challenges of human existence, the magnificent universe and the unknown future ahead in this terrific twenty-first century and beyond. It affirms that life is but a blink of an eye.

(12) Reflections, Recollections & Expressions:

135

Collected Essays bring forth author's point of views on education, religions, human nature and how to build an enlightened society in the present century and more.

Appendix C

Readership Reviews

★★★★☆ **This book offers a brief look at the path to ...**
October 3, 2016

This book offers a brief look at the path to self-realization and an awakened universe At a time when nations are caught up in war, communal hatred and injustices this books conveys optimism about how to forge universal brotherhood and mindfulness in our life. Dr.Bhatt calls for early training of children in morality and ethics consistent with Vedantic values so as to develop character and mindset necessary for a higher conscious...Read More

View on Amazon.com Add a comment View this book's reviews on Amazon.com

<u>Yoshi</u> **reviewed** <u>Magnificent Quest: Life, Death &</u>
<u>Eternity</u>

★★★★★ **A spectacular read! May 31, 2016**

This is the second book I have read by this author, and again, I am blown away by the knowledge here. This book delves into the essence of life and its many questions and really stirred something within my mind. It brings forth many pertinent ideas and presents them in such a way as to really hold your attention. I could not put this book down.

A very interesting read. Definitely worth your while!

<u>Yoshi</u> **reviewed** <u>Triumph of the Bold: A Poetic Reality</u>

★★★★★ **Inspirational and full of vision! May 31, 2016**

A deep and thought-provoking book. A definite must-read!

★★★★☆ **Odyssey of the Dammed - Revolving Destiny July 16, 2013**

In an age where space exploration has enhanced the possibility of detecting life on other planets in the universe, comes this fascinating story of Neandro, an earthling, vs Dr Godseed, a super enlightened alien and his conniving cohorts.

Intrigue and menace through changes in time and space make for an intricate plot with a cast of unforgettable characters.

Will Col. James Neanderson (AKA Neandro) make...Read More

★★★★★ A road map to evolution March 1, 2013

Here in a small compact book is an outline of where we have come from, with road map for future evolution.
Dr Bhatt has done a great service by distilling the wisdom of the past and defining how to move ahead.
Now, it is up to all of us to take advantage of it and follow the right path.

141

<u>Rajam</u> reviewed <u>Rolling Spirits: Being Becoming</u>

★★★★★ **Rolling Spirits; Poems December 11, 2012**

It was very interesting. It is written in 3 parts.

In his own words these poems are a gift to the 21st generations to explore, to introspect, to reflect upon human challenges,struggles,triumphs and much more to know who we are and what we can become.

In the second part he is saying that humans are the masters of their destiny.

A lot of the poems reflect his hope for global peace &unity.
<br...<u>Read More</u> </br...

<u>View on Amazon.com</u> <u>Add a comment</u> <u>View this book's reviews on Amazon.com</u>

145

<u>Joseph M.</u> **reviewed** <u>Human Endeavor : Essence & Mission: A Call for Global Awakening</u>

★★★★★ **A tender feeling August 29, 2012**

A delightful and heartwarming collection of the memories, insights and emotions of Dr. Bhatt's life journey. His engaging, yet vulnerable way with language, will evoke gratitude for the simple joys and meaningful relationships of our lives.

<u>View on Amazon.com</u> <u>Add a comment</u> <u>View this book's reviews on Amazon.com</u>

146

Rolling Sprit is poems related to our daily life experiences of love, marriage, broken heart, and some light effect like getting ticket, family and many other aspects in life we encounter. Some of the verses are worth remembering or reading the again.

I loved the book and recommend reading it.

147

<u>manohar N</u> **reviewed** <u>Human Endeavor :
Essence & Mission: A Call for Global
Awakening</u>

★★★★☆ **HUMAN HISTORY May 21, 2011**

**I CONSIDERED MYSELF AN EDUCATED MAN,
UNTIL I READ THIS BOOK. IN A COMPACT
FORM, THE AUTHOR HAS PROVIDED
WEALTH OF KNOWLEDGE ABOUT OUR VERY
EXISTENCE. THE BOOK HAS WOVEN
TOGETHER SEVERAL DISCIPLINES IN A
FASHION NOT SEEN BEFORE. RELIGION,
PHILOSOPHY, HISTORY, MOLECULAR
BIOLOGY, AND EVOLUTION, ARE ALL VERY
DIFFICULT SUBJECTS TO COMPREHEND. BUT
ONE GETS A BREADTH OF KNOWLEDGE AND
A BIRDS EYE VIEW ABOUT HUMAN
ENDEAVOR, IN THIS...**<u>Read More</u>

<u>View on Amazon.com</u> <u>Add a comment</u> <u>View this
book's reviews on Amazon.com</u>

153

<u>mambao</u> reviewed <u>Human Endeavor : Essence & Mission: A Call for Global Awakening</u>

★★★★★ a good read May 2, 2011

This is a thought provoking book. The author calls for a global awakening at an individual level to a more peaceful society. He ties together the various religious, philosophical and scientific traditions from both Eastern and Western cultures as a base for our shared human experience. Then he proposes a new mode of thinking as the way forward.

The book is enjoyable and interesting with collected wisdom and quotes...<u>Read More</u>

<u>View on Amazon.com</u> <u>Add a comment</u> <u>View this book's reviews on Amazon.com</u>

154

Human Endeavor : Essence & Mission: A Call for Global Awakening

★★★★★ **Very insightful...thought provoking** April 2, 2011

A great read...introduces you to various religious and scientific ideas in an easily readable and not overwhelming way...easy to follow....as you read the book you gather information so that you understand the main goals and ideas in the final chapters...highly recommend.